WORLD

SWEDEN
FINLAND
ESTONIA
LATVIA
LITHUANIA
ND
POLAND
CZECH
SLOVAKIA
AUSTRIA HUNGARY
ROMANIA
ITALY
BULGARIA
GREECE
GEORGIA
AZERBAIJAN
TURKEY
NISIA
CYPRUS
SYRIA
ISRAEL
JORDAN IRAQ
LIBYA
EGYPT
ER
CHAD
SUDAN
CAMEROON
CENTRAL
AFRICAN
REPUBLIC
ABON
CONGO
RWANDA
UGANDA
BURUNDI
KENYA
TANZANIA
ANGOLA
ZAMBIA
MALAWI
ZIMBABWE
MOZAMBIQUE
NAMIBIA
BOTSWANA
SWAZILAND
SOUTH
AFRICA
LESOTHO
MADAGASCAR

RUSSIA

KAZAKHSTAN

CASPIAN
SEA
TURKMENISTAN

IRAN
Kabul
AFGHANISTAN
PAKISTAN

KUWAIT
BAHRAIN
U.A.E
SAUDI
ARABIA
OMAN
YEMEN

SOMALIA
ETHIOPIA

MONGOLIA
Gobi Desert

CHINA

NORTH KOREA
Beijing
SOUTH KOREA
JAPAN
Tōkyō

NEPAL
BANGLA-
DESH
INDIA
MYANMAR
LAOS
Hong Kong
TAIWAN

HAINAN
BOAO

THAILAND
Bangkok
VIETNAM
CAMBODIA
PHILIPPINES

BRUNEI

MALAYSIA
SINGAPORE

PACIFIC

OCEAN

INDIAN

OCEAN

INDONESIA

PAPUA NEW GUINEA

TUVALU

Kakadu
National Park

AUSTRALIA

SOUTHERN OCEAN

NEW ZEALAND

40
60
80
100
120
140
160
180
80

60

40

20

20

40

60

80

40
60
80
100
120
140
160
180

Meet the World 2024

English through Newspapers

Edited with Notes

by

Yasuhiko Wakaari

写真提供

AFP/アフロ

株式会社山本海苔店

国立研究開発法人 宇宙航空研究開発機構（JAXA）

八丈町・八丈島観光協会・東京海洋大学鯨類学研究室

森永乳業株式会社

読売新聞社

立命館大学

協力

株式会社ローソン

音声ファイルのダウンロード／ストリーミング

CD マーク表示がある箇所は、音声を弊社 HP より無料でダウンロード／ストリーミングすることができます。下記 URL の書籍詳細ページに音声ダウンロードアイコンがございますのでそちらから自習用音声としてご活用ください。

https://www.seibido.co.jp/ad693

Meet the World 2024
English through Newspapers

はしがき

● はじめに

　この教科書を手にしたみなさんの中には、「テレビやインターネット、スマホがあるこの時代になぜわざわざ新聞を読まなくてはいけないの？」と疑問に思う人がいるかもしれません。確かにテレビは新聞と比べて娯楽性や臨場感に優れていますし、インターネットには膨大な情報量とこれまでのメディアにはなかった「双方向性」があります。また携帯電話やスマートフォンの普及によって、世間の注目を集める試合や選挙の結果はほぼリアルタイムで、しかも検索しなくても分かるようになりました。

　では新聞はもう必要ないのでしょうか。いいえ、そんなことはありません。情報技術が発達した現在だからこそ、実は新聞が必要なのではないでしょうか。

　みなさんがすでに普段の生活で体験しているように、現代社会にはさまざまな情報があふれています。例えばインターネットの検索エンジンに「英字新聞」と入力すると193万件が、「新聞」に至っては約6億件がヒットします。

　このように情報が氾濫している状況では、情報の取捨選択を行い、選択した情報に基づいて行動することが必要になります。では情報の取捨選択で一番大切なことは何でしょうか。

　これについてはさまざまな意見があるかもしれませんが、情報で最も重要なのはその「信頼性」だと思います。いくら早く手に入れることができても、信頼性に欠ける情報であればそれを基に行動するのは危険と言えます。福島第一原発の事故や新型コロナウイルスの感染拡大、ワクチン接種やロシアによるウクライナ侵攻が始まった時期に流れたさまざまな情報はそのことを私たちに教えてくれたのではないでしょうか。

　新聞は、現在の多様化したメディアの中で、最も信頼性が高いことが各種調査で明らかになっています。他のメディアに比べ記録性に優れていることがその証拠と言えるでしょう。新聞を読み、信頼性の高い情報を基に行動する習慣を身に付けることは、みなさんがこれから自分の将来を選択する上でとても重要になります。

本書の目的と特徴

　本書は「英語はある程度読めるけれど英字新聞はほとんど読んだことがない」という方を対象とした教材です。本書の目的は3つあります。一つは英字新聞に慣れ親しんでもらうこと、もう一つは英字新聞を読むためのノウハウを身に付けてもらうこと、そして最後にみなさんの身のまわりで起こっているさまざまな出来事に興味を持ってもらうことです。それぞれの目的に関して本書で工夫した点をいくつか紹介します。

● 1 英字新聞に慣れ親しんでもらうこと

　みなさんは英語の文章を訳したときに「なんとか日本語にできたけど内容はほとんど分からなかった」という経験をしたことはないでしょうか。これにはいくつかの理由がありますが、「文

章の背景状況が分からない」ことが大きな要因として考えられます。

　本書では、Before reading において記事と関連する情報を提示したり、記事を理解する上で重要な語句を確認するタスクを設けています。これらのタスクを行うことで、「内容に関する背景知識があれば、英文記事の内容理解はそれほど難しくない」ことが実感できるでしょう。

　また収録した記事は、語数を基本にしつつ、トピックや場面のわかりやすさにも配慮して配列しています。本書での学習を通じて、最初は「長い」と感じていた記事にもいつの間にか抵抗なく取り組めるでしょう。

● ② 英字新聞を読むためのノウハウを身につけてもらうこと

　英字新聞の理解には、内容に関する背景知識の理解に加え、記事の形式、つまり新聞英語の構成や特徴の理解も重要です。

　本書ではみなさんにこのようなノウハウを身につけてもらうために、新聞英語の特徴を要点ごとにコラムにまとめ、本書の Unit 1 ～ 10 で紹介しています。またコラムの内容理解を助けるためのタスクを設け、記事を読みながら形式について少しずつ理解できるよう配慮しました。さらに巻頭の iii ～ v では新聞英語の特徴をまとめて掲載しています。

● ③ 現在の社会で起こっている様々な出来事に興味を持ってもらうこと

　本書では、現在の社会で起こっているさまざまな出来事に目を向けることができるよう、*The Japan News* 紙等から日本で起きた出来事と海外発の記事をバランスよく収録しています。またこの種の教材としては多めの 20 の記事を収録しました。特に AI の活用やポストコロナの取り組みなど、みなさんの現在や今後の生活に関わる話題を多く取り上げています。

　もし本書の中にみなさんの興味を引く記事を見つけたら、ぜひ関連する情報を調べてみてください。記事に関する知識が深まると同時に、もっと多くのことを知りたいと思うようになるでしょう。そういう興味・関心を持つことがみなさんの将来の進路を決める意外なきっかけになるかもしれません。

● おわりに

　本書の作成にあたっては多くの方のご協力をいただきました。秋田大学の学生のみなさんには有益なアドバイスを、また成美堂の中澤ひろ子氏をはじめとするスタッフの方々にも大変お世話になりました。この場をお借りして厚くお礼申し上げます。

編著者記す

新聞英語の特徴

• いろいろな読み方に対応した記事の構成

　本や雑誌に比べ、新聞はいろいろな読み方をされます。時間をかけて全ての記事を熟読することもあれば、特定の記事だけを読んだり、記事の最初の部分にさっと目を通すだけのこともあります。新聞記事は最初の部分しか読まなくても要点が把握できるよう、Headline（見出し）、Lead（前文）、Body（本文）の3つで構成されています。

• **Headline** の特徴① スペースの効率的利用

　広告のコピーライティングと同様、新聞記事の Headline は、「短く、鋭く、気の利いた」（Short, Sharp, Snappy）表現で読者の目を引くように、また限られたスペースでもメッセージを効率的に伝えられるようにさまざまな工夫をしています。例えば、(1) 冠詞、(2) 特別動詞（BE, HAVE）、(3) 接続詞（and, that）、(4) 文の終わりのピリオド、といったメッセージの意味内容に大きく関わらない語や記号は基本的に省略されます。また、(5) 略語、(6) 縮約語、(7) つづりの短い語、のような省スペースの表現が多用されます。

• **Headline** の特徴② 時制の変化

　Headline では is, were といった BE 動詞や has, had のような HAVE 動詞が省略されるなど、通常の英語とは異なった時制表現が用いられます。具体的には、(1)「現在完了」の表現と「過去形」は「現在形」に、(2)「受身」の表現は「過去分詞」だけに、(3)「BE 動詞 +-ing」（進行中、または現在から見て実現の可能性が極めて高いことを示す表現）は「現在分詞 (-ing)」だけに、(4)「BE 動詞 +going to+ 動詞の原形」（現時点で可能性が高いことを示す表現）は「to+ 動詞の原形」だけになります。

通常の英語では	新聞英語では
過去形	現在形
[HAVE] + 過去分詞	
[BE] + 過去分詞	過去分詞
[HAVE] been + 過去分詞	
[BE] + [DO]ing	現在分詞
[BE] + going to + 動詞の原形	to +動詞の原形

• Headline の特徴③ 句読点の使用

すでに述べたように、Headline では and, that といった接続詞が省略され、代わりにコンマ (,) が使われます。またコロン (:) やセミコロン (;) にも接続詞や一部の前置詞の代わりをする働きがあります。コロンは誰かの発言や補足説明、セミコロンは前半部分と後半部分が何らかのつながりを持っていることを示します。具体的には、前半の内容について後半でその理由を挙げて説明したり、前半と後半の内容が対照的であることなどを意味します。

• Headline の特徴④ 略語、縮約語の使用

すでに述べたように、Headline では IMF, NATO, IOC, WHO のような略語や、Dept., S'pore といった縮約語が多用されます。縮約語は Dept. や ad. のように語の最後にピリオド (.) がついたり、S'pore や int'l のようにアポストロフィ (') がつくことが多く、読み手はそれらの記号によって縮約語であると知ることができます。しかし記事によっては dept や intl のように、そのような記号さえも省略されることがあります。

• Headline の特徴⑤ つづりの短い語の使用

同じような意味を表わす語が 2 つ以上ある場合、Headline ではつづりの短い方を用います。例えば「援助する」の意味を表わす語には aid や assist、「問題」には issue や problem などの語がありますが、新聞英語では特別な事情がない限り短い方の aid や issue が使用されます。

• Headline の特徴⑥ 簡潔な表現の問題点

すでに述べたように、Headline ではメッセージの意味内容と大きく関連しない機能語（例：特別動詞や接続詞）を省略したり、省スペースの表現（例：縮約語やつづりの短い語）を多用するなど、メッセージを効率的に示す工夫をしています。他方で、機能語の省略や省スペース表現の多用はいろいろな解釈を可能にするという問題を伴います。例えば新聞英語の現在形は過去形と現在完了の両方の解釈ができます。また Rep. という縮約語は Republican（[米国の] 共和党員）にも Representative（[米国の] 下院議員）にも解釈できます。こういった場合の判断には Headline 全体またはその先の Lead や Body まで読むことが重要です。

• Lead の特徴

記事全文のうち最初の部分を Lead（前文）と言います。Lead は記事の書き出しであると同時に記事全文の要約でもあります。Lead には「5W1H」、つまり Who, What, When, Where, Why, How（誰が、何を、いつ、どこで、なぜ、どのように）に関する情報が簡潔に含まれていて、この部分を読むだけで記事の要旨が理解できます。Lead は読み手、特に記事に最後まで目を通す時間のない人にとって大切な役割を担っています。

• **Body** の特徴

　記事全文のうち Lead を除く部分を Body（本文）と言います。Body は通常複数の段落から構成され、Headline や Lead で示された要点を詳しく説明する役割を担っています。Body の段落は情報の核心部分（＝重要度が高い部分）から順に配列され、段落が下がるに従って補足的、周辺的（＝重要度が低い）になっていきます。このような段落構成を「逆三角形型」または「逆ピラミッド型」（inverted pyramid style）と呼びますが、この構成は読み手にとって情報を効率的に把握できるメリットが、書き手にとっては記事の分量を調整する際に書き直す手間が省けるメリットがあります。

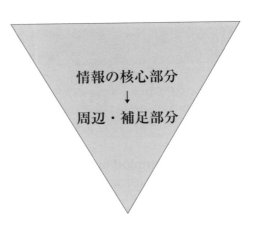

情報の核心部分
↓
周辺・補足部分

• その他の新聞英語の特徴

　新聞英語に見られるその他の特徴として、次の2つを挙げることができます。

　　① 発言者・報告者の名前は発言・報告内容の後に置かれることが多い。
　　　　例1："... ChatGPT ... had ... organization and composition," <u>the authors wrote</u>.
　　　　例2："... ChatGPT ... was somewhat repetitive," <u>Choi wrote</u>.

　　② 補足説明の挿入が多い。
　　　　例1：Jonathan Choi, <u>a professor at Minnesota University Law School</u>, gave ...
　　　　例2：" ... strategy," said Manabu Murata, <u>an international education commentator</u>.

　これらの特徴は、限られたスペースの中で読み手が効率的に要点を把握できるよう配慮した結果生まれたと考えられます。

■ CONTENTS

Unit の構成

　本書は、リーディングを中心に、リスニングやスピーキング、ライティングなどの技能を総合的に育成することをねらいとしており、各 Unit は Before reading 1 及び 2, While reading 1 ～ 5, After reading 1 ～ 3 の 10 のタスクで構成されています。それぞれのタスクのねらいは以下の通りです。

・Before reading 1 ： 背景知識を与えることでトピックに対する興味や理解を促したり、トピックと関連する語句を確認するタスク。
・Before reading 2 ： 専門用語のように、文脈からの推測も難しい語句などの意味を確認するタスク。

・While reading 1 ： 情報を整理するノート・テイキングのタスク。
・While reading 2 ： 文章から特定の情報を探し出す、スキャニングのタスク。
・While reading 3 ： 文章の要点をすくい取って全体の大意を理解する、スキミングを意識した要約完成のタスク。
・While reading 4 ： CD を聞き、完成した要約や全体の大意を確認するリスニングのタスク。
・While reading 5 ： 行間を読み取らせる推論発問により読解力を高めるタスク。

・After reading 1 ： 語句を並べ替える英作文により文法力を鍛えるタスク。
・After reading 2 ： 定義をヒントに文中から単語を抜き出すことで語の意味を確認するタスク。
・After reading 3 ： 記事のトピックに関する考えを深めると同時に、自分の意見やアイデアをメモにまとめることでライティングの力を養うタスク。メモを参考に口頭で発表することでスピーキングの力を高めることにもつながります。

コラム

UNIT 1

ChatGPT bot passes U.S. law school exam

ChatGPT ボットが米国法科大学院の試験に合格

みなさんは ChatGPT を利用したことがありますか？ この人工知能チャットボットは、人間の質問に対し、自然な文章で回答を生成することから注目を集めています。この Unit では、ChatGPT が米国法科大学院の試験に合格したことを報じた記事を紹介します。

🔲 Before reading 1

説明を読み、内容に関する理解を深めましょう。
また表からどんなことが言えるか考えてみましょう。

-ChatGPT は、米国企業（U.S. company）の OpenAI が 2022 年 11 月に公開した人工知能（artificial intelligence）のチャットボット

	ChatGPT	Bing Chat	Bard
提供主体	OpenAI	Microsoft	Google
利用規約上の年齢制限	13 歳以上 18 歳未満の場合は保護者同意	成年であること 未成年の場合は保護者同意	18 歳以上
利用料	GPT3.5 の場合は無料 GPT4 の場合は 20 米ドル / 月	無料	無料

出典：「初等中等教育段階における生成 AI の利用に関する暫定的なガイドライン」（文部科学省）を加工して作成

(chatbot) です。chatbot は、「会話（chat）」と「ロボット（robot）」の略語 bot を組み合わせた言葉で、ユーザーからの質問に自動で返答してくれるプログラムを意味します。

- 米国ミネソタ大学の法科大学院（law school）の試験問題は、多肢選択問題（multiple-choice question）と作文問題（essay question）で構成されています。

🔲 Before reading 2

日本語に対応する英語表現を選択肢から選び、○で囲みましょう。

1. 共著者　　　　　coauthor / coeditor

2. 憲法　　　　　　administrative law / constitutional law

3. 課税　　　　　　taxation / taxonomy

4. 不法行為　　　　toad / tort

5. 管轄区域　　　　jurisdiction / justification

1

ChatGPT bot passes U.S. law school exam

①PARIS (AFP-Jiji) — A chatbot powered by reams of data from the internet has passed exams at a U.S. law school after writing essays on topics ranging from constitutional law to taxation and torts.

5 ②ChatGPT from OpenAI, a U.S. company that last month got a massive injection of cash from Microsoft, uses artificial intelligence (AI) to generate streams of text from simple prompts.

③The results have been so good that educators have warned
10 it could lead to widespread cheating and even signal the end of traditional classroom teaching methods.

④Jonathan Choi, a professor at Minnesota University Law School, gave ChatGPT the same test faced by students, consisting of 95 multiple-choice questions and 12 essay
15 questions.

⑤In a white paper titled "ChatGPT goes to law school" published on Jan. 23, he and his coauthors reported that the bot scored a C+ overall.

⑥While this was enough for a pass, the bot was near the
20 bottom of the class in most subjects and "bombed" at multiple-choice questions involving mathematics.

'Not a great student'

⑦"In writing essays, ChatGPT displayed a strong grasp of
25 basic legal rules and had consistently solid organization and composition," the authors wrote.

⑧But the bot "often struggled to spot issues when given an open-ended prompt, a core skill on law school exams."

⑨Officials in New York and other jurisdictions have banned
30 the use of ChatGPT in schools, but Choi suggested it could

---

reams of ～ たくさんの～

injection 注入、投入

prompt 刺激するもの、促すもの

Jonathan Choi ジョナサン・チョイ氏

bombed 失敗した（米国の学生が使う俗語）

be a valuable teaching aid.

⑩"Overall, ChatGPT wasn't a great law student acting alone," he wrote on Twitter.

⑪"But we expect that collaborating with humans, language
35 models like ChatGPT would be very useful to law students taking exams and to practicing lawyers."

⑫And playing down the possibility of cheating, he wrote in reply to another Twitter user that two out of three markers had spotted the bot-written paper.

40 ⑬"[They] had a hunch and their hunch was right, because ChatGPT had perfect grammar and was somewhat repetitive," Choi wrote.

practicing lawyer 開業
弁護士、実務弁護士
play down ～ ～を軽く
扱う、～を軽視する

🔎 While reading 1　次に関して、記事を読んで分かったことをメモしましょう。

1.　米国ミネソタ大学の法科大学院の試験問題

....

....

2.　ChatGPT の試験の成績

....

....

3.　Jonathan Choi 氏の発言

....

....

....

📝 column　｜ いろいろな読み方に対応した記事の構成

本や雑誌に比べ、新聞はいろいろな読み方をされます。時間をかけて全ての記事を熟読することも
あれば、特定の記事だけを読んだり、記事の最初の部分にさっと目を通すだけのこともあります。
新聞記事は最初の部分しか読まなくても要点が把握できるよう、Headline（見出し）、Lead（前文）、
Body（本文）の３つで構成されています。

Task　この **Unit** の記事の **Headline**、**Lead**、**Body** をそれぞれ○で囲みましょう。

記事の中で次の情報が述べられている段落の番号を書きましょう。

1. OpenAI 社に多額の資金を投入した企業：[   ]

2. Jonathan Choi 氏の所属：[   ]

3. ChatGPT の総合成績：[   ]

4. ボットが書いた答案を見つけた採点者の数：[   ]

⊗ **While reading 3**
空欄に適切な単語または数字を入れ、記事の要約を完成させましょう。
答えが単語の場合、最初の文字がヒントとして示してあります。

ChatGPT is a chatbot powered by reams of data from the internet and uses [1)]a_____ intelligence to generate streams of text from simple prompts. A professor at Minnesota University [2)]L_____ School gave the bot the same test faced by students. In a white paper titled "ChatGPT goes to law school" published on January [3)]_____, 2023, the professor and his coauthors reported that the bot scored a C+ overall. While this was enough for a [4)]p_____, the bot was near the bottom of the class in most subjects and "bombed" at multiple-choice questions involving [5)]m_____.

⊗ **While reading 4**
3 で空欄に入れた単語または数字が正しいか、音声で確認しましょう。

🔊 1-06

⊗ **While reading 5**
記事が示唆する内容と合致すれば T、しなければ F を記入しましょう。

1. Microsoft provided OpenAI with cash in January, 2022. [   ]

2. Educators are worried that ChatGPT could be used for cheating. [   ]

3. The test ChatGPT took had a total of more than 100 questions. [   ]

4. Students in New York are allowed to use ChatGPT in schools. [   ]

語句を並べ替えて英文を完成させましょう。間違った場合、解答欄に正しい答えを書くこと。

1. OpenAI 社は Microsoft 社から大量の資金投入を受けた。

   OpenAI (of / got / cash / from / Microsoft / a massive injection).

   予 想 : ....

   解 答 : *OpenAI*

   ....

2. 私たちは ChatGPT が実務弁護士にとって役立つだろうと期待している。

   We expect that (be / to / would / useful / ChatGPT / practicing lawyers).

   予 想 : ....

   解 答 : *We expect that*

   ....

3. 教育者たちは伝統的な教室での指導方法がもはや適切ではないかもしれないと警告している。

   Educators (no longer / may / have / that / warned / traditional classroom teaching methods) be appropriate.

   予 想 : ....

   解 答 : *Educators*

   .... *be appropriate.*

4. 作文試験でのトピックの範囲は憲法から課税や不法行為にまで及んだ。

   Topics (in / to / from / ranged / constitutional law / the essay exam) taxation and torts.

   予 想 : ....

   解 答 : *Topics*

   .... *taxation and torts.*

 **After reading ②** 次の説明はどの語についてのものか、文中から抜き出して必要に応じ 正しい形に直しましょう。最初の文字がヒントとして示してあります。

1. an action that is wrong but not criminal and can be dealt with in a civil court of law

2. an addition of money to something in order to improve it

3. the science of numbers and of shapes, including algebra, geometry, and arithmetic

4. to say that something must not be done, seen, used, etc.

5. to notice someone or something, especially when they are difficult to see or recognize

6. a feeling that something is true even though you do not have any evidence to prove it

| 1. t _____ | 2. i _____ | 3. m _____ |
| 4. b _____ | 5. s _____ | 6. h _____ |

 **After reading ③** 次の課題について、自分の考えを述べましょう。

あなたは ChatGPT の利用制限に賛成ですか、反対ですか。またそう思う理由は何ですか。あなたの考えを書いてみましょう。

日本語でのメモ

英語での作文

UNIT 2

Smiley, dimpled sphinx statue unearthed in Egypt

えくぼのある笑顔のスフィンクス像、エジプトで発見

 みなさんはテレビや写真で「スフィンクス像」を見たことはありますか？ もしある場合、像がどんな表情をしているか覚えていますか？ この **Unit** では、えくぼのあるめずらしいスフィンクス像がエジプトで発見されたことを報じた記事を取り上げます。

🔲 Before reading 1

説明を読み、内容に関する理解を深めましょう。
また図からどんなことが言えるか考えましょう。

- スフィンクス（sphinx）は、ライオンの身体と人間の頭を持つ神話的存在で、起源はエジプト（Egypt）にあると言われています。
- 同国の観光地としては、三大ピラミッドのあるギザ（Giza）、考古学博物館のある首都カイロ（Cairo）、王家の谷があるルクソール（Luxor）が有名です。
- 同国の経済は観光業（tourism industry）に依存（count on）しており、政府（government）は旅行客（tourists）を呼び寄せ（draw in）ようとしています。

海外からの渡航者数（単位：万人）

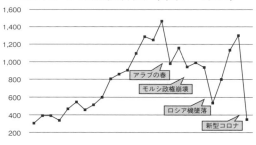

出所：世界銀行、考古・観光省よりジェトロ作成
（https://www.jetro.go.jp/biz/areareports/2021/966aea43b2aa0d32.html）

🔲 Before reading 2

日本語に対応する英語表現を選択肢から選び、○で囲みましょう。

1. 考古学者　　archaeologist / anthropologist

2. えくぼ　　dimple / dumpling

3. 観光・考古省　the tourism and antiquark ministry / the tourism and antiquities ministry

4. 文化遺物　　artefact / artifice

5. 石碑　　steel / stele

Smiley, dimpled sphinx statue unearthed in Egypt

①Archaeologists in Egypt have unearthed a sphinx statue with a smiley face and two dimples near the Hathor Temple, one of the country's best preserved ancient sites, the tourism and antiquities ministry announced Monday.

Hathor Temple　ハトホル神殿

5 ②It is the latest in a series of discoveries revealed over the past few months.

③The limestone artefact, believed to be a stylised representation of an ancient Roman emperor, was found inside a two-level tomb near the temple in southern Egypt,
10 the ministry said in a statement.

④Next to the beautifully and accurately carved sphinx, researchers had found a Roman stele written in demotic and hieroglyphic scripts, the ministry's statement said.

demotic　（古代エジプトの）民衆文字の
hieroglyphic　（古代エジプトの）象形文字の

⑤Once fully deciphered, the stele may shed light on the
15 identity of the sculpted ruler, who the Egyptian research team said could be Emperor Claudius.

Emperor Claudius　皇帝クラウディアス（ローマ帝国第4代皇帝）

⑥Hathor Temple, about 500 kilometres south of the capital, Cairo, was home to the Dendera Zodiac, a celestial map which has been displayed at the Louvre in Paris since 1922,
20 more than a century after Frenchman Sebastien Louis Saulnier had blasted it out of the temple.

Dendera Zodiac　デンデラの黄道帯

Sebastien Louis Saulnier　セバスチャン・ルイ・ソルニア

⑦Egypt wants it back.

⑧The country has unveiled major archaeological discoveries in recent months, primarily in the Saqqara necropolis south
25 of Cairo but also in Giza, home of the only surviving structure of the seven wonders of the ancient world.

Saqqara necropolis　サッカラの埋葬地

⑨On Thursday, the antiquities ministry announced the discovery of a hidden nine-metre passage inside the Great Pyramid of Giza, which archaeologist Zahi Hawass said may
30 lead to the actual burial chamber of pharaoh Khufu, or

Zahi Hawass　ザヒ・ハワス氏

pharaoh Khufu　クフ王

Cheops.
⑩Further south, in Luxor, archaeologists had discovered an 1,800-year-old complete residential city from the Roman era, authorities announced in January.
⑪Some experts see such announcements as having more political and economic weight, than scientific, as Egypt is counting on tourism to revive its vital tourism industry amid a severe economic crisis.
⑫The government aims to draw in 30 million tourists a year by 2028, up from 13 million before the pandemic.

Cheops ケオプス（Khufu のギリシア語名）

While reading 1

次に関して、記事を読んで分かったことをメモしましょう。

1. スフィンクス像と像が発見された場所

2. 最近のエジプトにおけるその他の発見

column　Headline の特徴① スペースの効率的利用

広告のコピーライティングと同様、新聞記事の Headline は「短く、鋭く、気の利いた」（Short, Sharp, Snappy）表現で読者の目を引くように、また限られたスペースでメッセージを最も効率的に伝えられるようにさまざまな工夫をしています。例えば、①冠詞、②特別動詞（BE, HAVE）、③接続詞（and, that）、④文の終わりのピリオド、といったメッセージの意味・内容に大きく関わらない語や記号は基本的に省略されます。また、⑤略語、⑥縮約語、⑦つづりの短い語、のような省スペースの表現が多用されます。

Task　次の 3 つの Headline を分析し、基になる英文を作ってみましょう。

(1) 7 Earth-size planets found
(2) Lack of oxygen hurting corals in world's oceans
(3) DiCaprio, pope discuss environment

1. エジプト観光・考古省が像の発見に関する発表を行った曜日：[   ]

2. 首都カイロからハトホル神殿までの距離：[   ]

3. ギザの大ピラミッドの内部にある隠れ通路の長さ：[   ]

4. エジプト政府が 2028 年までに目標としている年間観光客数：[   ]

⊗ **While reading 3** 空欄に適切な単語または数字を入れ、記事の要約を完成させましょう。答えが単語の場合、最初の文字がヒントとして示してあります。

On March 6, 1)_____, the tourism and antiquities ministry announced that archaeologists in Egypt had unearthed a sphinx 2)s_____ with a smiley face and two dimples near the Hathor Temple. The limestone artefact was found inside a two-level tomb near the temple in 3)s_____ Egypt. Next to the beautifully and accurately carved sphinx, researchers had found a Roman stele written in demotic and hieroglyphic 4)s_____. Once fully deciphered, the stele may shed light on the identity of the sculpted ruler, who the Egyptian research team said could be 5)E_____ Claudius.

⊗ **While reading 4** 3で空欄に入れた単語または数字が正しいか、音声で確認しましょう。

🔊 1-11

⊗ **While reading 5** 記事が示唆する内容と合致すれば T、しなければ F を記入しましょう。

1. The Dendera Zodiac was originally in the capital, Cairo. [   ]

2. The Dendera Zodiac has been away from Egypt for more than a century. [   ]

3. The seven wonders of the ancient world have lost their original shape except the Great Pyramid of Giza. [   ]

4. The government aims to more than double the number of tourists by 2028 compared to before the pandemic. [   ]

 **After reading 1** 語句を並べ替えて英文を完成させましょう。間違った場合、解答欄に 正しい答えを書くこと。なお文頭に来る語句も小文字にしてあります。

1. その像は神殿の近くにある２層構造の墓の中で見つかった。

(was / near / found / inside / the statue / a two-level tomb) the temple.

予想 : ....

....

解答 : ....

the temple.

2. デンデラの黄道帯は 1922 年からパリのルーブルに展示されている。

The Dendera Zodiac (at / in / has / been / displayed / the Louvre) Paris since 1922.

予想 : ....

解答 : *The Dendera Zodiac* ....

Paris since 1922.

3. 研究者たちは美しく彫られた像の隣にローマ時代の石碑を発見した。

(to / next / found / researchers / a Roman stele / the beautifully carved statue).

予想 : ....

....

解答 : ....

....

4. ピラミッド内にあるその隠し通路は、クフ王の玄室につながっている可能性がある。

The hidden passage (to / may / lead / inside / the pyramid / the burial chamber) of pharaoh Khufu.

予想 : ....

解答 : *The hidden passage* ....

of pharaoh Khufu.

11

1. an ancient Egyptian stone statue of a creature with a human head and the body of a lion lying down

2. a small hollow place on your skin, especially one on your cheek or chin when you smile

3. to find the meaning of something that is difficult to read or understand

4. an area of land where dead people are buried, especially a large ancient one

5. to become healthy and strong again, or to make someone or something healthy and strong again

6. a disease that affects people over a very large area or the whole world

1. s _____	2. d _____	3. d _____
4. n _____	5. r _____	6. p _____

After reading 3 次の課題について、自分の考えを述べましょう。

あなたが観光してみたい国はどこですか。またその国に行きたい理由は何ですか。あなたの考えを書いてみましょう。

日本語でのメモ

英語での作文

UNIT 3

Gender pay progress stalls on 'motherhood penalty'—study

男女間賃金格差は「母親ペナルティー」で停滞―研究で明らかに

みなさんは男女間の賃金格差がどれくらいあるか知っていますか？　また賃金格差の原因について考えたことはありますか？　この **Unit** では、賃金格差の解消が進まない最大の要因を明らかにした研究について取り上げた記事を紹介します。

🔲 Before reading 1

説明を読み、内容に関する理解を深めましょう。
また図からどんなことが言えるか考えましょう。

- プライスウォーターハウスクーパーズ (PwC) は会計監査、税務、法務等を総合的に手がける世界的コンサルティング企業 (consultancy) です。

-PwC の報告書は、賃金格差 (pay gap) の要因が出産 (childbirth) 後の子育て (raising children) による生涯賃金 (lifetime earnings) の損失にあると結論づけています。

男女間賃金格差の推移

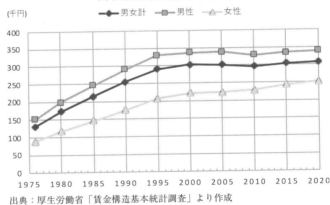

（千円）　　―◆―男女計　―■―男性　―△―女性

出典：厚生労働省「賃金構造基本統計調査」より作成

🔲 Before reading 2

日本語に対応する英語表現を選択肢から選び、○で囲みましょう。

1. 時給　　　　　　hourly earnings / hourly expenses

2. ジェンダー公正　gender parity / gender polity

3. 不完全就業　　　unemployment / underemployment

4. 育児休暇　　　　parental leave / maternity leave

5. 年次指数　　　　annual index / biannual index

Gender pay progress stalls on 'motherhood penalty'— study

①There has been minimal global movement toward gender pay equality because many women still face a motherhood penalty after having children, a study said Tuesday.

②Progress has been exceedingly slow in industrialized
5　nations over the past decade, consultancy PricewaterhouseCoopers (PwC) said in a report using the latest available 2021 data.

③The average pay gap between men and women, in terms of median hourly earnings, stands at 14 percent and has
10　only narrowed by 2.5 percentage points since 2011, according to PwC's Women in Work Index.

Women in Work Index
「働く女性インデックス」

④It would take half a century to reach gender parity at this rate, the group said, adding recent improvements were driven by post-Covid recovery rather than genuine progress.

15　⑤The motherhood penalty — the loss in lifetime earnings experienced by women raising children — has become the most significant driver of the gender pay gap, PwC concluded in its report.

⑥Prompted by the underemployment and slower career
20　progression women experience on returning to work after childbirth, it is perpetuated by the unfair share of childcare women take on in almost every country around the world.

take on〜　〜を引き受ける

⑦In Britain, gender inequality was exacerbated by a childcare affordability crisis and the low take-up by fathers of shared
25　parental leave, the report said.

⑧Affordable childcare is critical in helping to ease the pressure on mothers and families, and reduce women's unpaid care load.

⑨This needs to be complemented with policy solutions that aim to redistribute unpaid childcare more equally between
30　women and men.

⑩Luxembourg topped PwC's annual index, which rates the

performance of OECD nations using key metrics for women's employment outcomes.

⑪The second best performer was New Zealand, followed by Slovenia.

⑫"If the rebound from Covid-19 has taught us anything, it is that we can't rely on economic growth alone to produce gender equality — unless we want to wait another 50 years or more," said PwC economist Larice Stielow.

Larice Stielow ラリーチェ・スティロー氏

⑬"We must design and develop policy solutions that actively address the underlying causes of the inequality that exist today," she added.

⑭Britain stood at 14th place, but was the top G7 nation ahead of Canada (18), Germany (21), France (23), the United States (25), Japan (28) and Italy (30).

 **While reading 1**　次に関して、記事を読んで分かったことをメモしてみましょう。

1. PwC の報告書の内容

2. PwC のエコノミストの発言

---

column　　**Headline の特徴② 時制の変化**

Headline では is, were といった BE 動詞や has, had のような HAVE 動詞が省略されるなど、通常の英語とは異なった時制表現が用いられます。具体的には、①「現在完了」の表現と「過去形」は「現在形」に、②「受身」の表現は「過去分詞」だけに、③「BE 動詞 +-ing」（進行中、または現在から見て実現の可能性が極めて高いことを示す表現）は「現在分詞 (-ing)」に、④「BE 動詞 +going to+ 動詞の原形」（現時点で可能性が高いことを示す表現）は「to+ 動詞の原形」になります。

通常の英語では	新聞英語では
過去形	①
[HAVE] + 過去分詞	
[BE] + 過去分詞	②
[HAVE] been + 過去分詞	
[BE] + [DO]ing	③
[BE] + going to + 動詞の原形	④

Task　上の表の ①〜④ に適切な表現を入れ、表を完成させましょう。

1. 時給の中央値における男女間の平均賃金格差：[　　　]

2. 英国において男女間の賃金格差が広がった要因：[　　　]

3. PwC の年次指数で最上位にランクされた国：[　　　]

4. PwC の年次指数における日本の順位：[　　　]

According to PwC's Women in Work Index, the average pay gap between men and women, in terms of median hourly earnings, stands at [1)]_____ percent and has only narrowed by 2.5 percentage points since [2)]_____. The report concluded that the most significant driver of the gender pay gap is the motherhood [3)]p_____ — the loss in lifetime earnings experienced by women raising children. Prompted by the [4)]u_____ and slower career progression women experience on returning to work after childbirth, it is perpetuated by the unfair share of [5)]c_____ women take on in almost every country around the world.

🔊 1-16

1. The average pay gap between men and women, in terms of median hourly earnings, was more than 16% in 2011. [　　　]

2. According to PwC, if there is no drastic change, gender parity will not be achieved until 2070. [　　　]

3. According to PwC, genuine progress in gender pay equality has been reflected in recent improvements. [　　　]

4. According to PwC's annual index, the gender pay gap was smaller in Japan than in Italy. [　　　]

語句を並べ替えて英文を完成させましょう。間違った場合、解答欄に正しい答えを書くこと。なお文頭に来る語句も小文字にしてあります。

1. 男女間の賃金格差の平均は 2011 年から 2.5 パーセント縮まっている。

The average pay gap between men (by / and / has / women / narrowed / 2.5 percentage points) since 2011.

予 想 : ....

解 答 : *The average pay gap between men* ....

.... *since 2011.*

2. 英国では、男女間の不平等は父親の共有育児休暇の取得率の低さによって悪化した。

In Britain, gender inequality (by / by / was / fathers / exacerbated / the low take-up) of shared parental leave.

予 想 : ....

解 答 : *In Britain, gender inequality* ....

.... *of shared parental leave.*

3. 手頃な価格の育児は女性の無給の育児負担を軽減する上で重要である。

Affordable childcare (in / is / to / reduce / helping / critical) women's unpaid care load.

予 想 : ....

解 答 : *Affordable childcare* ....

.... *women's unpaid care load.*

4. 近年の改善は真の進歩によってもたらされたものではなかった。

(by / not / were / driven / recent improvements / genuine progress).

予 想 : ....

....

解 答 : ....

....

 **After reading 2**　次の説明はどの語についてのものか、文中から抜き出して必要に応じ正しい形に直しましょう。最初の文字がヒントとして示してあります。

1. very small in degree or amount, especially the smallest degree or amount possible

2. something bad that happens to you because of something you have done or because of the situation you are in

3. a company that gives expert advice on a particular subject to other companies or organizations

4. being the middle number or measurement in a set of numbers or measurements that have been arranged in order

5. to make a situation, attitude, etc., especially a bad one, continue to exist for a long time

6. to add to something in a way that improves it or makes it more attractive

1. m＿＿＿＿＿	2. p＿＿＿＿＿	3. c＿＿＿＿＿
4. m＿＿＿＿＿	5. p＿＿＿＿＿	6. c＿＿＿＿＿

After reading 3　次の課題について、自分の考えを述べましょう。

男女の賃金格差を減らすために、どのような取り組みが必要だと思いますか。またその取り組みが重要と思う理由は何ですか。あなたの考えを書いてみましょう。

日本語でのメモ

英語での作文

UNIT 4

Sea ice in Antarctic at record low—US data center

南極の氷、観測史上最小に—米データセンター

地球温暖化の問題は近年様々なメディアで取り上げられていますが、みなさんはこの問題についてどのくらい知っているでしょうか？　この Unit では、南極の海氷面積が観測史上最小になったことを報じた記事を取り上げます。

Before reading 1

説明を読み、内容に関する理解を深めましょう。
また図からどんなことが言えるか考えましょう。

- 南極の氷は夏に溶け（thaw）、冬に凍る（freeze）サイクルを繰り返しています。
- 南極の海氷（sea ice）面積は45 年前から人工衛星（satellite）による観測が行われていました。今回の氷の縮小（shrink）と地球温暖化の関連は明らかになっていません。

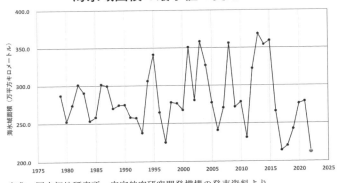

1979 ～ 2022 年の各年の南極海における
海氷域面積の最小値の変動

出典：国立極地研究所、宇宙航空研究開発機構の発表資料より

Before reading 2

日本語に対応する英語表現を選択肢から選び、○で囲みましょう。

1. 北極圏　　　　　Arctic / Arctica

2. 南極大陸　　　　Antarctica / Antiarctica

3. 地球温暖化　　　global warming / global worming

4. 氷床　　　　　　ice seat / ice sheet

5. 大陸　　　　　　continent / continence

Sea ice in Antarctic at record low—US data center

①Antarctic sea ice likely shrunk to a record low last week, US researchers said Monday, its lowest extent in the 45 years of satellite record-keeping.

②The National Snow and Ice Data Center (NSIDC) at the University of Colorado Boulder said that Antarctica's sea ice fell to 1.79 million square kilometers (691,000 million square miles) on February 21.

③That exceeded the previous record low set in 2022 by 136,000 square kilometers (52,500 square miles).

④NSIDC scientists stressed that the latest figure was preliminary since further late-season melt was still possible. They said they would issue a final number on the extent of ice in early March.

⑤Melting sea ice exposes the thicker ice shelves buttressing Antarctica's ground ice sheet to waves and warmer temperatures.

⑥Melting sea ice has no discernible impact on sea levels because the ice is already in ocean water.

⑦But the sea ice rings Antarctica's massive ice shelves, the extensions of the freshwater glaciers that threaten catastrophic sea level rise over centuries if they continue melting as global temperatures rise.

⑧"Antarctica's response to climate change has been different from the Arctic's," said Ted Scambos, a senior research scientist at the Cooperative Institute for Research in the Environmental Sciences (CIRES).

⑨"The downward trend in sea ice may be a signal that global warming is finally affecting the floating ice around Antarctica, but it will take several more years to be confident of it," Scambos said.

---

record low 最低記録、最小記録

National Snow and Ice Data Center 国立雪氷データセンター

University of Colorado Boulder コロラド大学ボルダー校

buttress 補強する

discernible 認識できる、認められる

Ted Scambos テッド・スカンボス氏

senior research scientist 上席科学研究員

Cooperative Institute for Research in the Environmental Sciences 環境科学研究共同研究所

⑩The Antarctic cycle undergoes significant annual variations during its summers of thawing and winters of freezing, and the continent has not experienced the rapid melting of the past four decades that plague the ice sheets of Greenland

35 and the Arctic due to global warming.

plague 〜を苦しめる、〜に災いする

⑪But the high melt rate since 2016 raises concerns that a significant downward trend may be taking hold.

take hold 定着する、確立する

⑫Melting of the sea ice is problematic because it helps accelerate global warming.

40 ⑬When white sea ice — which bounces up to 90 percent of the Sun's energy back into space — is replaced by dark, unfrozen sea, the water absorbs a similar percentage of the Sun's heat instead.

⑭Globally, last year was the fifth or sixth warmest on record

45 despite the cooling influence of a natural La Niña weather pattern.

La Niña ラ・ニーニャ（赤道付近の東太平洋、ペルーやエクアドルの沖合の広い範囲で海面水温が低くなる現象）

🔊 *While reading* **1**　次に関して、記事を読んで分かったことをメモしましょう。

1.　国立雪氷データセンターの発表及びセンターの研究員の発言

2.　Ted Scambos 氏の発言

📃 column　　Headline の特徴③ 句読点の使用

すでに述べたように、Headline では and, that といった接続詞が省略され、代わりにコンマ (,) が使われます。またコロン (:)、セミコロン (;) にも接続詞や一部の前置詞の代わりをする働きがあります。コロンは誰かの発言や補足説明、セミコロンは前半部分と後半部分が何らかのつながりを持っていることを示します。具体的には、前半の内容について後半でその理由を挙げて説明したり、前半と後半の内容が対照的であることなどを意味します。

Task　次の 3 つの記事の Headline にあるコロン (:) は何を表わしているか、考えてみましょう。

(1) Oxfam: 8 men as rich as half the world

(2) 'Vegetable steel' : Bamboo as ecologically-friendly building material

(3) U.K. court: Richard III to be buried in Leicester

記事の中で次の情報が述べられている段落の番号を書きましょう。

1. 人工衛星による記録が行われている年数：[   ]

2. 国立雪氷データセンターが発表を行った日：[   ]

3. Ted Scambos 氏の所属：[   ]

4. 白い海氷が太陽のエネルギーを反射する割合：[   ]

⊗ **While reading 3**　空欄に適切な単語または数字を入れ、記事の要約を完成させましょう。答えが単語の場合、最初の文字がヒントとして示してあります。

On February 21, 2023, the 1)N_____ Snow and Ice Data Center at the University of Colorado Boulder said that Antarctica's sea ice fell to 2)_____ million square kilometers. The figure exceeded the previous record low set in 2022 by 3)_____ square kilometers. Scientists at the center stressed that the latest figure was preliminary since further late-season melt was still possible. Melting of the sea ice is problematic because it helps accelerate 4)g_____ warming. When white sea ice is replaced by dark, unfrozen sea, the water absorbs the Sun's 5)h_____ at a much higher rate.

⊗ **While reading 4**　3 で空欄に入れた単語または数字が正しいか、音声で確認しましょう。

🔊 1-21

⊗ **While reading 5**　記事が示唆する内容と合致すれば T、しなければ F を記入しましょう。

1. Antarctica's sea ice was less than 1.90 million square kilometers in 2022. [   ]

2. According to NSIDC scientists, the final figure on the extent of ice could be less than 1.79 million square kilometers. [   ]

3. Ted Scambos is confident that the downward trend in Antarctic sea ice is caused by global warming. [   ]

4. Antarctic sea ice has been melting at a high rate for more than five years. [   ]

語句を並べ替えて英文を完成させましょう。間違った場合、解答欄に
正しい答えを書くこと。なお文頭に来る語句も小文字にしてあります。

1. NSIDC の科学者たちは、3月上旬に氷の大きさに関する最終的な数字を発表予定だと述べた。

NSIDC scientists said they (of / on / issue / would / the extent / a final number)
ice in early March.

予 想 : ....

....

解 答 : *NSIDC scientists said they*

ice in early March.

2. 海氷の溶解によって、より厚い氷棚が波やより高い気温にさらされる。

(to / and / waves / exposes / melting sea ice / the thicker ice shelves) warmer
temperatures.

予 想 : ....

....

解 答 : ....

warmer temperatures.

3. 海氷の溶解は地球温暖化の加速に貢献する。

(of / helps / melting / accelerate / sea ice / global warming).

予 想 : ....

....

解 答 : ....

.

4. 白い海氷は太陽のエネルギーのほとんどを宇宙にはね返す。

White sea ice (of / back / into / most / bounces / the Sun's energy) space.

予 想 : ....

....

解 答 : *White sea ice*

space.

 **After reading 2** 次の説明はどの語についてのものか、文中から抜き出して必要に応じ正しい形に直しましょう。最初の文字がヒントとして示してあります。

1. happening before something that is more important, often in order to prepare for it

2. to support or give strength to somebody/something

3. a large mass of ice, formed by snow on mountains, that moves very slowly down a valley

4. sure that something will happen in the way that you want or expect

5. to cause pain, suffering, or trouble to someone, especially for a long period of time

6. to happen or to make something happen faster or earlier than expected

1. p _____	2. b _____	3. g _____
4. c _____	5. p _____	6. a _____

After reading 3 次の課題について、自分の考えを述べましょう。

地球温暖化を防ぐために、どのような取り組みが必要だと思いますか。またその取り組みが必要だと思う理由は何ですか。あなたの考えを書いてみましょう。

日本語でのメモ

英語での作文

24

UNIT 5

Hachijojima aims to make splash with whale watching

八丈島、ホエールウォッチングを観光の目玉に

伊豆諸島の一つ、八丈島。みなさんは八丈島にどんなイメージを持っていますか。この Unit では、コロナ禍で観光客数が落ち込んでいる状況を改善しようと、八丈島が行った取り組みを報じた記事を紹介します。

Before reading 1

説明を読み、内容に関する理解を深めましょう。
また図からどんなことが言えるか考えましょう。

- 東京都に属する八丈島 (Hachijojima Island) は都心 (central Tokyo) から約 290km 南に位置して (located) います。一島で八丈町を形成し、町の人口 (population) は約 7,000 人です。

- ザトウクジラ (humpback whale) は 2015 年から八丈島周辺でも目撃される (sighted) ようになりました。

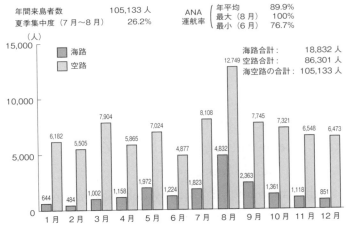

航路別来島者数の月別推移 (平成 27 年 1 月~12 月)

年間来島者数	105,133 人	ANA 運航率	年平均	89.9%
夏季集中度 (7 月~8 月)	26.2%		最大 (8 月)	100%
			最小 (6 月)	76.7%

海路合計: 18,832 人
空路合計: 86,301 人
海空路の合計: 105,133 人

提供：八丈町役場

Before reading 2

日本語に対応する英語表現を選択肢から選び、○で囲みましょう。

1. 壊滅　　　　　wipeout / breakout

2. 見世物　　　　specter / spectacle

3. 大使　　　　　ambusher / ambassador

4. 生態学　　　　ecology / ethnology

5. 中断、途絶　　discretion / disruption

Hachijojima aims to make splash with whale watching

①After suffering a tourism wipeout during the pandemic, Hachijojima Island has found a new spectacle to get its visitors back: whale watching. In addition to working with Mizuho Bank, Ltd. to develop an artificial intelligence-based system for monitoring humpback whales, the local government is seeking to attract tourists from overseas with its first non-Japanese tourism ambassador. ②Located about 290 kilometers south of central Tokyo, the island is blessed with a mild climate and tourist draws such as hot springs.

③According to the town's industry and tourism department, the number of tourists to the island in fiscal 2019 reached about 87,000. That number dropped to about 39,000, or by roughly 50%, in fiscal 2020, when the novel coronavirus spread across the world and caused major disruptions to travel. In fiscal 2021, the number stood at about 51,000, still far below the pre-pandemic level.

④To help pull in more tourists to the island, the government for the town of Hachijo, which has jurisdiction over the island, set its sights on whale watching, which has been gaining popularity in recent years.

⑤Humpback whales are often spotted around Okinawa Prefecture and the Ogasawara Islands between November and May of each year, and since 2015, they have also been sighted around Hachijojima. The marine mammals can even be seen directly from the island, without the need to first board a boat. In fact, many tourists to the island, as they drive around or bathe in hot springs, have seen the whales jump up out of the ocean and into the air.

写真：八丈島近海に現れたザトウクジラ

写真提供：八丈町・八丈島観光協会・東京海洋大学鯨類学研究室

Mizuho Bank, Ltd. 株式会社みずほ銀行

industry and tourism department 産業観光課

Hachijo 八丈
jurisdiction 管轄区

Ogasawara Islands 小笠原諸島

⑥The town has been studying the ecology and population of humpbacks jointly with Tokyo University of Marine Science and Technology, among other institutions.

Tokyo University of Marine Science and Technology 東京海洋大学

AI for observation

⑦The town government has signed an agreement with Mizuho Bank, which operates a branch office on the island, for support in promoting the island's digital transformation in a wide range of fields, including disaster prevention and tourism.

branch office 支店

disaster prevention 防災

⑧Under the agreement, which also covers the study of whales locally, the town will increase the number of observation cameras installed on the island from one to five, and use an AI system to recognize splashes caused by whales in order to inform tourists of the whales' location.

⑨Meanwhile, the town is keeping a close eye on the global tourism industry as it recovers, hoping to attract visitors from overseas. (From The Japan News)

keep a close eye on ~ ~を注視する

 **While reading 1** 次に関して、記事を読んで分かったことをメモしましょう。

1. 八丈島を訪れる観光客数の推移について

....

2. ザトウクジラについて

....

---

column | **Headline の特徴④ 略語、縮約語の使用**

すでに述べたように、Headline では IMF, NATO, IOC, WHO のような略語や、Dept., S'pore といった縮約語が多用されます。縮約語は Dept. や ad. のように語の最後にピリオド(.)がついたり、S'pore や int'l のようにアポストロフィ (') がつくことが多く、読み手はそれらの記号によって縮約語であると知ることができます。しかし記事によっては dept や intl のように、そのような記号さえも省略されることがあります。

Task 次の 4 つの記事の Headline で縮約されている部分を○で囲み、元の形を書いてみましょう。

(1) U.N. says world eating too much sugar
(2) Dalai Lama calls for intl investigation
(3) 'Low-cost airfare era' to begin this yr?
(4) Govt to set target for '50 emissions

⊗ While reading 2
記事の中で次の情報が述べられている段落の番号を書きましょう。

1. 東京都心から八丈島までの距離：[   ]

2. 2021 年の観光客数：[   ]

3. ザトウクジラの生態等を八丈町と共同で研究している大学の名前：[   ]

4. 八丈島に設置される予定の観測カメラの台数：[   ]

⊗ While reading 3
空欄に適切な単語または数字を入れ、記事の要約を完成させましょう。
答えが単語の場合、最初の文字がヒントとして示してあります。

Located about ¹⁾_____ kilometers south of central Tokyo, Hachijojima Island is blessed with a mild climate and tourist ²⁾d_____ such as hot springs. However, after the novel coronavirus caused major disruptions to travel, the number of tourists has been far ³⁾b_____ the pre-pandemic level. Thus, to help pull in more tourists to the island, the government for the town of Hachijo set its sights on ⁴⁾w_____ watching, which has been gaining popularity in recent years. The marine mammals can even be seen directly from the island, without the need to first ⁵⁾b_____ a boat.

⊗ While reading 4
3 で空欄に入れた単語または数字が正しいか、音声で確認しましょう。

🔊 1-26

⊗ While reading 5
記事が示唆する内容と合致すれば T、しなければ F を記入しましょう。

1. Compared to fiscal 2019, the number of tourists to Hachijojima decreased more than 30% in fiscal 2021. [   ]

2. People in Okinawa can see humpback whales in summer. [   ]

3. About 20 years ago, many people in Hachijojima saw humpback whales directly from the island. [   ]

4. Four more observation cameras will be installed on the island of Hachijojima. [   ]

語句を並べ替えて英文を完成させましょう。間違った場合、解答欄に正しい答えを書くこと。

1. 2021 年度の観光客数はパンデミック前の水準を下回った。

The number (in / of / was / below / tourists / fiscal 2021) the pre-pandemic level.

予想 : ....

解答 : *The number* ....

the pre-pandemic level.

2. ホエールウォッチングは近年非常に人気になっている。

Whale watching (of / has / been / gaining / popularity / a lot) in recent years.

予想 : ....

解答 : *Whale watching* ....

in recent years.

3. 鯨が空中に飛び上がるのを多くの観光客が目撃している。

Many tourists (up / have / into / jump / seen / the whales) the air.

予想 : ....

解答 : *Many tourists* ....

the air.

4. 町は鯨が起こす波しぶきを認識する人工知能システムを活用予定だ。

The town will (to / use / caused / splashes / recognize / an AI system) by whales.

予想 : ....

解答 : *The town will* ....

by whales.

1. a very large animal that lives in the sea and looks like a fish, but is actually a mammal

2. a person who acts as a representative or promoter of a specified activity

3. a situation in which something is prevented from continuing in its usual way

4. the relation of plants and living creatures to each other and to their environment; the study of this

5. an arrangement or promise to do something, made by two or more people, companies, organizations, etc.

6. a local office or shop/store belonging to a large company or organization

1. w _____	2. a _____	3. d _____
4. e _____	5. a _____	6. b _____

After reading 3 次の課題について、自分の考えを述べましょう。

離島への観光客数を増やすために、どういった取り組みが必要だと思いますか。またその取り組みが必要だと思う理由は何ですか。あなたの考えを書いてみましょう。

日本語でのメモ

英語での作文

Prototype spacesuit for future NASA mission to Moon unveiled

将来の月探査計画用宇宙服の試作品がお目見え

 みなさんは宇宙旅行に興味はありますか？ 宇宙服を着てみたいと思ったことはありますか？ この Unit では、米航空宇宙局が次期の月探査計画で使用する次世代宇宙服の試作品が公開されたことを報じた記事を取り上げます。

Before reading 1

説明を読み、内容に関する理解を深めましょう。
また図からどんなことが言えるか考えましょう。

- 米航空宇宙局（NASA）のアポロ計画（Apollo missions）で、人類が最初に月面（lunar surface）に着陸したのは 1969 年です。アルテミス計画（Artemis program）は、最終的な目標である有人火星（Mars）探査の第一段階（initial step）と位置づけられています。

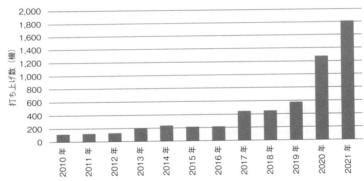

世界の人工衛星の打ち上げ数

（資料）UNITED NATIONS Office for Outer Space Affairs 公表資料
出典：経済産業省ウェブサイト
(https://www.meti.go.jp/statistics/toppage/report/minikaisetsu/hitokoto_kako/20220722hitokoto.html)

Before reading 2

日本語に対応する英語表現を選択肢から選び、○で囲みましょう。

1. 宇宙飛行士　　　　astronaut / astrologer

2. 試作品　　　　　　prototype / platinotype

3. 宇宙用語　　　　　space jargon / space javelin

4. 独自設計　　　　　property design / proprietary design

5. 可動範囲　　　　　range of motion / range of motive

Prototype spacesuit for future NASA mission to Moon unveiled

①NASA and the private aerospace company Axiom Space unveiled a prototype on Wednesday of the next-generation spacesuit that astronauts will wear on the next walk on the Moon.

⑤②The suit revealed at an event at the Johnson Space Center in Houston features greater flexibility and thermal protection than those worn by the Apollo astronauts who first stepped foot on the lunar surface more than 50 years ago.

③The pressurized garment has multiple protective layers, a ⑩ backpack with life support systems, and lights and a high-definition video camera mounted on top of the bubble-shaped helmet.

④The US space agency's Artemis program aims to return humans to the Moon in late 2025 for the first time since the ⑮ historic Apollo missions ended in 1972, an initial step towards an eventual voyage to Mars.

⑤Axiom Space was awarded a $228.5 million contract to design the suit — the Axiom Extravehicular Mobility Unit in space jargon — for the mission known as Artemis III.

⑳⑥Axiom Space chief engineer Jim Stein appeared on stage at the NASA facility wearing the suit, waving his arms, performing squats and dropping to one knee to display the range of motion it provides.

⑦The spacesuit modeled by Stein featured a cover layer in ㉕ all black with blue and orange trim which Axiom Space said was required to conceal the suit's proprietary design.

⑧The final version will be in the traditional white used to reflect heat from the Sun and protect astronauts from the temperatures of the harsh lunar environment.

㉚⑨The suit features a backpack Axiom Space described as a

Axiom Space アクシオムスペース

Johnson Space Center ジョンソン宇宙センター
Houston ヒューストン
Apollo アポロ（月着陸計画に用いられた米国の3人乗り宇宙船）

high-definition 高精細度の、高解像度の

Artemis program アルテミス計画（月に人類の活動拠点を築くことを主目的とする有人月探査計画）

Axiom Extravehicular Mobility Unit Axiom 船外活動ユニット
Artemis III アルテミス3（アルテミス計画の第3段階で、男女の宇宙飛行士が月面に降り立つことを目指している）
Jim Stein ジム・スタイン氏

portable life support system.

⑩"Inside of this box are all the parts and the components to keep you alive," said Russell Ralston, deputy program manager for extravehicular activity at Axiom Space.

35 ⑪"You can think of it as like a very fancy scuba tank and air conditioner kind of combined into one."

⑫The suit is designed to be worn for up to eight hours at a time.

⑬It features multiple layers — an inner layer called a bladder layer that holds air inside the spacesuit like a balloon and a

40 restraint layer that maintains its shape.

⑭An insulation layer made of different fabrics protects the astronauts against the huge temperature fluctuations on the Moon while the outer layer is designed to be resistant to dust and potential tears from sharp rocks.

Russell Ralston　ラッセル・ラルストン氏
deputy program manager　副プログラムマネージャー

a restraint layer　拘束層

An insulation layer　断熱層

◎ While reading 1　次に関して、記事を読んで分かったことをメモしましょう。

1.　Russel Ralston 氏の発言

....

2.　宇宙服を構成する複数の層とその役割

....

⊜ column　**Headline の特徴⑤ つづりの短い語の使用**

同じような意味を表わす語が 2 つ以上ある場合、Headline ではつづりの短い方を用います。例えば「援助する」の意味を表わす語には aid や assist、「問題」には issue や problem などの語がありますが、新聞英語では特別な事情がない限り短い方の aid や issue が使用されます。

Task　次の 3 つの Headline で使われている単語のうち、新聞英語に特徴的なものを○で囲んでみましょう。

(1) White hackers eyed for cyberdefense
(2) Obama moves to tighten gun control
(3) France moves to ban ultrathin models

1. ジョンソン宇宙センターがある場所：[　　　]

2. アポロ計画が終了した年：[　　　]

3. Russel Ralston 氏の役職：[　　　]

4. 1回（の活動）において宇宙服が着用できる時間の上限：[　　　]

On March 15, 2023, NASA and the private aerospace company Axiom Space unveiled a ¹⁾p_____ of the next-generation spacesuit that astronauts will wear on the next walk on the Moon. The suit revealed at an event at the Johnson Space Center in Houston features greater ²⁾f_____ and thermal protection than those worn by the Apollo astronauts who first stepped foot on the lunar surface more than ³⁾_____ years ago. The pressurized garment has multiple protective layers, a ⁴⁾b_____ with life support systems, and lights and a high-definition video camera mounted on top of the bubble-shaped ⁵⁾h_____ .

1. The Apollo astronauts stepped foot on the lunar surface in the 1980s.
   [　　　]

2. Nobody has stepped foot on the lunar surface since the Apollo astronauts did.
   [　　　]

3. Astronauts who will walk on the Moon in late 2025 will wear the black spacesuit with blue and orange trim.　[　　　]

4. The next-generation spacesuit will enable astronauts to work outside the spaceship for more than half a day without a break.　[　　　]

語句を並べ替えて英文を完成させましょう。間違った場合、解答欄に正しい答えを書くこと。なお文頭に来る語句も小文字にしてあります。

1. その宇宙服は、アポロ計画の宇宙飛行士が着ていたものよりも優れた柔軟性が特徴である。

The spacesuit (by / than / worn / those / features / greater flexibility) the Apollo astronauts.

予想：

解答： *The spacesuit*

the Apollo astronauts.

2. 外装は宇宙服の独自設計を隠すために必要だった。

(to / was / conceal / required / the outer layer / the spacesuit's proprietary design).

予想：

解答：

3. 宇宙飛行士を月の厳しい環境から守るために伝統的な白が用いられる予定だ。

The traditional white (be / to / used / will / protect / astronauts) from the harsh lunar environment.

予想：

解答： *The traditional white*

from the harsh lunar environment.

4. 内側の層は宇宙服の中で気球のように空気を保持する。

(air / like / holds / inside / the spacesuit / the inner layer) a balloon.

予想：

解答：

a balloon.

1. the first form that a new design of a car, machine, etc., has, or a model of it used to test the design before it is produced

2. many, or involving many things, people, events, etc.

3. a strong hard hat that soldiers, motorcycle riders, the police, etc., wear to protect their heads

4. relating to work performed in space outside a spacecraft

5. words and expressions used in a particular profession or by a particular group of people, which are difficult for other people to understand

6. made and sold by a particular company and protected by a registered trademark

1. p ＿＿＿＿＿＿	2. m ＿＿＿＿＿＿	3. h ＿＿＿＿＿＿
4. e ＿＿＿＿＿＿	5. j ＿＿＿＿＿＿	6. p ＿＿＿＿＿＿

⚠ After reading 3   次の課題について、自分の考えを述べましょう。

あなたがもし宇宙に行くとしたら、宇宙服にどんな機能を求めますか。またその機能が必要だと 思う理由はなんですか。あなたの考えを書いてみましょう。

日本語でのメモ

英語での作文

UNIT 7

Most Coming-of-Age Day events stick with 20-year-olds

成人式の多くは対象が 20 歳のまま

みなさんは成人式を何歳の時にお祝いしたいと思いますか。この Unit では、成人年齢引き下げの一方、多くの自治体の成人式で対象年齢が変更されなかったことを報じた記事を紹介します。

Before reading 1 説明を読み、内容に関する理解を深めましょう。
また表からどんなことが言えるか考えましょう。

- 民法（Civil Code）の改正（revision）により、日本では成人年齢（legal age of adulthood）が 18 歳に引き下げられ（lowered）ましたが、自治体（municipality）の多くは式の対象者を 20 歳のままにしています。

18 歳（成年）になったらできること	20 歳にならないとできないこと（これまでと変わらないこと）
◆親の同意がなくても契約できる ・携帯電話の契約 ・ローンを組む ・クレジットカードをつくる ・一人暮らしの部屋を借りる　など ◆10 年有効のパスポートを取得する ◆公認会計士や司法書士、医師免許、薬剤師免許などの国家資格を取る ◆結婚 　女性の結婚可能年齢が 16 歳から 18 歳に引き上げられ、男女とも 18 歳に。 ◆性同一性障害の人が性別の取扱いの変更審判を受けられる ※普通自動車免許の取得は従来と同様、「18 歳以上」で取得可能	◆飲酒をする ◆喫煙をする ◆競馬、競輪、オートレース、競艇の投票券（馬券など）を買う ◆養子を迎える ◆大型・中型自動車運転免許の取得 

出典：政府広報オンライン
(https://www.facebook.com/gov.online/photos/a.342406255856335/2595860483844223/?locale=ms_MY) を加工して作成

Before reading 2 日本語に対応する英語表現を選択肢から選び、○で囲みましょう。

1. 大学入学共通テスト　　Common Test for University Diploma /

　　　　　　　　　　　　Common Test for University Admissions

2. 大学二年生　　sofomore / sophomore

3. 入学試験　　entrance exam / preliminary exam

4. 就職活動　　job seating / job searching

5. 保護者　　guardian / protractor

Most Coming-of-Age Day events stick with 20-year-olds

①The legal age of adulthood was lowered to 18 last year, but on Monday, many local municipalities across the nation stuck to the tradition of marking Coming-of-Age Day for those turning 20 this year.

②Some rebranded the event as "Hatachi no Tsudoi," or a "gathering of 20-year-olds."

③Of the 62 wards, cities, towns and villages in metropolitan Tokyo, a total of 59 limited their ceremonies to participants who will become 20 this year, according to a survey conducted by The Yomiuri Shimbun.

④Tokyo's Koto Ward was among those that retained the traditional age for its ceremony at the local Tiara Koto hall. About 2,400 participants, some dressed in colorful kimono, joyfully reunited with friends and former classmates with exchanges of "Long time no see" and "Congratulations."

⑤But instead of calling it the "Seijin-shiki" (Coming-of-Age Ceremony) for its 20-year-olds, the ward changed the title this year to "Hatachi no Tsudoi" in light of the new legal age of adulthood, which was lowered to 18 with a revision of the Civil Code in April last year.

⑥"The ceremony made me realize the support that I've received in my life from my parents and many people around me," said a 20-year-old ward resident, currently a university sophomore. "I'm happy to celebrate this milestone."

⑦Among the reasons given for keeping the ceremony for 20-year-olds was that for 18-year-olds, "it coincides with university entrance exams or job searching, which places a

写真：成人式（2023 年）
写真提供：AFP/ アフロ

Coming-of-Age Day
成人の日

Hatachi no Tsudoi 二十歳のつどい

The Yomiuri Shimbun
読売新聞
Koto Ward　江東区
Tiara Koto　ティアラこうとう

Seijin-shiki　成人式

large burden on the participants and their guardians," according to Shibuya Ward.

⑧Like Koto Ward, about 50 municipalities in Tokyo held such ceremonies under the new name this year.

35 ⑨January is indeed a busy time for 18-year-olds as they prepare for the next stage in their lives. In particular, those preparing to take the Common Test for University Admissions on Jan. 14-15 would likely be unable to take the time to participate in the ceremony, even if one was held for

40 them.

⑩Still, some municipalities held their ceremonies in line with the new legal age as a way to encourage the new adults to be aware of their responsibilities.

⑪In Kunisaki, Oita Prefecture, the city government held a

45 ceremony for 20-year-olds on Aug. 14 and for 19-year-olds on Aug. 15 last year. It plans to hold one for 18-year-olds in May this year. (From The Japan News)

Shibuya Ward　渋谷区

Kunisaki　国東市

⊗ While reading 1　次に関して、記事を読んで分かったことをメモしましょう。

1.　成人式の対象を 20 歳にする自治体

....

2.　成人式の対象を 20 歳にする理由

....

While reading 2

記事の中で次の情報が述べられている段落の番号を書きましょう。

1. 東京都にある自治体の数：[　　　]

2. ティアラこうとうで行われた式典に参加した人数：[　　　]

3. 渋谷区が式典の対象者を 20 歳のままにした理由：[　　　]

4. 大学入学共通テストが実施される日：[　　　]

While reading 3

空欄に適切な単語または数字を入れ、記事の要約を完成させましょう。
答えが単語の場合、最初の文字がヒントとして示してあります。

The legal age of adulthood was lowered to ¹⁾_____ with a revision of the Civil Code in April, 2022, but many local municipalities across the nation retained the traditional ²⁾a_____ for their ceremonies. Among the reasons given for keeping the ceremony for 20-year-olds was that for 18-year-olds, January is a ³⁾b_____ time as they prepare for the next stage in their lives. In particular, those ⁴⁾p_____ to take the Common Test for University Admissions in the month would likely be unable to take the time to ⁵⁾p_____ in the ceremony, even if one was held for them.

While reading 4

3 で空欄に入れた単語または数字が正しいか、音声で確認しましょう。

🔊 1-36

While reading 5

記事が示唆する内容と合致すれば T、しなければ F を記入しましょう。

1. More than 90% of the municipalities in Tokyo retained the traditional age for their ceremonies.　[　　　]

2. Koto Ward held a ceremony called "Hatachi no Tsudoi" before the pandemic.　[　　　]

3. Many 18-year-olds will not be able to participate in the ceremony due to university entrance exams.　[　　　]

4. The city government of Kunisaki will likely hold a ceremony for 20-year-olds in 2023.　[　　　]

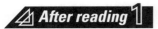 **After reading 1**　語句を並べ替えて英文を完成させましょう。間違った場合、解答欄に正しい答えを書くこと。なお文頭に来る語句も小文字にしてあります。

1. 参加者はかつての同級生と再会して「久しぶり」のやりとりをした。

The participants (were / with / with / reunited / exchanges / former classmates) of "Long time no see."

予想：
....
....

解答：　*The participants*
....
　　　　　　　　　　　　　　　　　　　　　　　　　of "Long time no see."

2. 就職活動は参加者とその保護者の負担になる。

(on / and / places / job searching / the participants / a large burden) their guardians.

予想：
....
....

解答：
....
　　　　　　　　　　　　　　　　　　　　　their guardians.

3. 多くの 18 歳は式典に参加する時間をとれない可能性が高い。

Many 18-year-olds would likely be (to / to / take / unable / participate / the time) in the ceremony.

予想：
....
....

解答：　*Many 18-year-olds would likely be*
....
　　　　　　　　　　　　　　　　　　　　in the ceremony.

4. 新成人に責任の自覚を促すために式典を開催した自治体もあった。

Some municipalities held their ceremonies to (be / of / to / aware / encourage / the new adults) their responsibilities.

予想：
....
....

解答：　*Some municipalities held their ceremonies to*
....
　　　　　　　　　　　　　　　　　　　　their responsibilities.

41

1. to change the image of a company or an organization or one of its products or services, for example by changing its name or by advertising it in a different way

2. one of the small areas that a city has been divided into for the purpose of local elections

3. to come together again or to bring people, parts of an organization, political party, or country together again

4. a student who is in their second year of study at a college or high school

5. a very important event in the development of something

6. a person who is legally responsible for the care of another person, especially a child whose parents have died

1. r _____	2. w _____	3. r _____
4. s _____	5. m _____	6. g _____

△ After reading 3　次の課題について、自分の考えを述べましょう。

あなたは成人式の対象を 18 歳と 20 歳のどちらにすべきだと思いますか。またそう思う理由は
何ですか。あなたの考えを書いてみましょう。

日本語でのメモ

英語での作文

UNIT 8

University campus security going high tech

大学キャンパスの警備、ハイテクに

みなさんは大学のキャンパスが安全だと感じていますか。この Unit では、大学周辺での相次ぐ刺傷事件を受け、キャンパスの警備にハイテク機器が利用されるようになったことを報じた記事を紹介します。

Before reading 1

説明を読み、内容に関する理解を深めましょう。
また図からどんなことが言えるか考えましょう。

- 政府の方針により、大学はコミュニティー機関（community institution）と位置づけられています。
- 多くの大学で地域住民（local resident）は食堂（cafeteria）や他の施設（facility）の利用ができます。
- 一方、一般への開放（open to the public）という方針がキャンパスの警備（campus security）を難しいものにしています。

防犯監視システムの整備率

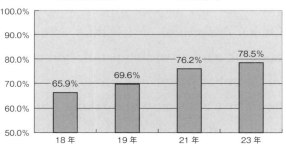

出典：文部科学省ホームページ
(https://www.mext.go.jp/b_menu/shingi/chukyo/chukyo3/077/siryo/_icsFiles/afieldfile/2016/10/25/1378368_9.pdf)

Before reading 2

日本語に対応する英語表現を選択肢から選び、○で囲みましょう。

1. 監視カメラ　　　candid camera / surveillance camera
2. 不法侵入　　　trepanning / trespassing
3. 立入禁止の　　　on-limits / off-limits
4. 社会学者　　　socialist / sociologist
5. 柱　　　pillar / pillager

University campus security going high tech

①Universities are preparing to turn to robots, artificial intelligence and drones to help with campus security following a spate of serious incidents resulting in injuries.

②Universities have become more vulnerable as they are expected to keep their campuses open to the public, so attention is being paid to how effective the latest technology is in quickly detecting suspicious activity and ensuring safety.

③Ritsumeikan University introduced a 1.3-meter tall egg-shaped patrol robot in 2021. The robot, which runs automatically, helps secure its Ibaraki Campus in Ibaraki, Osaka Prefecture, as it glides across the first floor of a building while avoiding people and pillars.

④The robot patrols the building at 1.4 kph for about two hours twice a day while taking 360-degree images of its surroundings. Even when it is not on patrol, it is constantly scanning the area, except for when it is charging.

⑤"When I'm on campus studying until late in the evening, it makes me feel a little safer to see the robot, even if I don't see other people on campus," said a 21-year-old female student.

⑥The school has also been testing AI-equipped surveillance cameras since December. When the cameras detect unusual behavior, such as violent acts or trespassing, the campus security control room is immediately notified. It has been reported that the system detected someone entering an area on campus that was off-limits.

⑦Human security guards are also patrolling the campus.

⑧"[The new tech] might be able to monitor areas that we can't

写真：校舎内をパトロールしている自律移動型警備ロボット
写真提供：立命館大学

a spate of 〜　多数の〜

Ritsumeikan University
立命館大学

Ibaraki Campus　（大阪）
いばらきキャンパス
Ibaraki　茨木市

campus security
control room　中央監視室

44

thoroughly check," said a 43-year-old campus security guard.

⑨Many universities allow local residents to freely enter their campuses, including their cafeterias and other facilities, as the government has positioned universities as community institutions.

⑩However, as campuses generally cover a large area, it is difficult for human guards to patrol the entire university. There is also the issue of aging guards.

⑪There have been several incidents on or around university campuses, including test-takers being stabbed in front of the University of Tokyo on the day of a major entrance exam in January 2022, as well as a sociologist and professor, being attacked at a Tokyo Metropolitan University campus in November.

⑫"AI and robots can significantly cut costs compared to hiring one security guard," said a Ritsumeikan University official. "We would like to create a safer campus by combining the latest technology [with conventional manpower]."
(From The Japan News)

Tokyo Metropolitan University 東京都立大学

⊗ **While reading 1**　次に関して、記事を読んで分かったことをメモしましょう。

1. 立命館大学が導入したロボットについて

....

2. ロボットや人工知能を搭載した監視カメラに関する人々の発言

....

≡ **column**　**Lead の特徴**

記事全文のうち最初の部分を Lead（前文）と言います。Lead は記事の書き出しであると同時に記事全文の要約でもあります。Lead には「5W1H」、つまり Who, What, When, Where, Why, How（誰が、何を、いつ、どこで、なぜ、どのように）に関する情報が簡潔に含まれていて、この部分を読むだけで記事の要旨が理解できます。Lead は読み手、特に記事に最後まで目を通す時間のない人にとって大切な役割を担っています。

Task　Unit 6（Prototype spacesuit for future NASA mission to Moon unveiled）の Lead（第一段落）を読み、5W1H のうちどの情報が含まれているかを確認しましょう。

記事の中で次の情報が述べられている段落の番号を書きましょう。

1. 立命館大学がパトロールロボットを導入した年：[　　　　]

2. ロボットが 1 日の間にパトロールを行う回数：[　　　　]

3. 43 歳の警備員の発言：[　　　　]

4. 東京都立大学で事件が起きた月：[　　　　]

⊗ **While reading 3** 空欄に適切な単語または数字を入れ、記事の要約を完成させましょう。
答えが単語の場合、最初の文字がヒントとして示してあります。

Many universities allow $^{1)}$l_____ residents to freely enter their campuses, including their cafeterias and other facilities, as the government has positioned universities as $^{2)}$c_____ institutions. However, as campuses generally cover a large area, it is difficult for human guards to patrol the entire university. There is also the issue of $^{3)}$a_____ guards. Furthermore, there have been several incidents on or around university campuses in $^{4)}$_____. Under such circumstances, universities are preparing to turn to robots, artificial intelligence and drones to help with campus $^{5)}$s_____.

⊗ **While reading 4** 3 で空欄に入れた単語または数字が正しいか、音声で確認しましょう。

🔊 **1-42**

⊗ **While reading 5** 記事が示唆する内容と合致すれば T、しなければ F を記入しましょう。

1. The robot introduced by Ritsumeikan University patrols the first floor of a building for more than five hours in total. [　　　　]

2. The AI-equipped surveillance cameras have been tested on campus for more than a year. [　　　　]

3. Local residents may use the campus cafeterias. [　　　　]

4. In general, more and more guards are becoming older. [　　　　]

語句を並べ替えて英文を完成させましょう。間違った場合、解答欄に
正しい答えを書くこと。なお文頭に来る語句も小文字にしてあります。

1. 大学はキャンパスを一般に開放することが期待されている。

Universities (to / are / keep / open / expected / their campuses) to the public.

予 想 : ....

解 答 : *Universities* ....

.... *to the public.*

2. 最新技術が安全確保にどれだけ効果的かに注目が集まっている。

Attention (is / to / how / paid / being / effective) the latest technology is in
ensuring safety.

予 想 : ....

解 答 : *Attention* ....

.... *the latest technology is in ensuring safety.*

3. ロボットは1日2回、約2時間ずつ建物をパトロールする。

(for / twice / patrols / the robot / the building / about two hours) a day.

予 想 : ....

....

解 答 : ....

.... *a day.*

4. 受験生が入試当日に大学の前で刺された。

Test-takers (in / of / were / front / stabbed / a university) on the day of an
entrance exam.

予 想 : ....

解 答 : *Test-takers* ....

.... *on the day of an entrance exam.*

 **After reading 2** 次の説明はどの語についてのものか、文中から抜き出して必要に応じ正しい形に直しましょう。最初の文字がヒントとして示してあります。

1. making you think that something bad or illegal is happening

2. the act of going to different parts of a building, an area, etc., to make sure that there is no trouble or crime

3. a tall upright round post used as a support for a roof or bridge

4. the act of carefully watching a person suspected of a crime or a place where a crime may be committed

5. a person, such as a soldier, a police officer or a prison officer, who protects a place or people, or prevents prisoners from escaping

6. following what is traditional or the way something has been done for a long time

---

1. s _____   2. p _____   3. p _____

4. s _____   5. g _____   6. c _____

After reading 3 次の課題について、自分の考えを述べましょう。

キャンパスの安全性を高めるために、どのような取り組みが必要だと思いますか。またその取り組みが必要だと思う理由は何ですか。あなたの考えを書いてみましょう。

日本語でのメモ

英語での作文

UNIT 9

Attending intl schools poses diploma questions

インターナショナルスクールへの登校、卒業資格の問題を提起

みなさんはインターナショナルスクールに通った経験はありますか。この Unit では、近年日本でのインターナショナルスクール開校が続く中、これらのスクールが法律上の「学校」と認められていないことから生じる問題について報じた記事を取り上げます。

Before reading 1

説明を読み、内容に関する理解を深めましょう。
また図からどんなことが言えるか考えましょう。

- 現在、日本には少なくとも 80 のインターナショナルスクール (international school) があると言われています。

- 中には全寮制学校（boarding school）もあり、学費（fee）は高額です。

- しかし、英語でレベルの高い教育 (high-level education) が受けられることから、特に所得の高い保護者 (parents with high incomes) のニーズを満たすものとなっています。

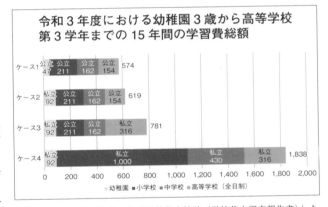

令和 3 年度における幼稚園 3 歳から高等学校第 3 学年までの 15 年間の学習費総額

出典：文部科学省「令和 3 年度学校基本統計（学校基本調査報告書）」より作成

Before reading 2

日本語に対応する英語表現を選択肢から選び、○で囲みましょう。

1. 公立学校　　　municipal school / independent school

2. 卒業生　　　　alumnus / aluminum

3. 有名人　　　　luminary / luminarist

4. 首相　　　　　prime minister / primate minister

5. 系列校　　　　affianced school / affiliated school

Attending intl schools poses diploma questions

①International schools are a growing presence in Japan amid burgeoning demand from parents seeking a full-fledged English-language education for their children. However, many such institutions are not regarded as ⁵ "schools" under Japanese law, so their students do not qualify for Japanese elementary or junior high school diplomas.

②In an effort to obtain diplomas for their children, some parents temporarily enroll their kids in Japanese municipal schools. But public school teachers are struggling to deal ¹⁰ with the situation and the government has not taken proactive steps to deal with the issue. Experts have called on the government to fully assess the situation and develop a system to evaluate the education that children receive at international schools.

¹⁵

¥9 mil. in annual fees

③An international school was established in Tohoku in August last year. It is a boarding school affiliated with a public school in the United Kingdom, whose alumni include ²⁰ such luminaries as a former British Prime Minister. About 180 individuals from 12 countries and regions enrolled in the school's first academic year, ranging from sixth-grade elementary schoolers to third year junior high school students. About 40% of the students are Japanese nationals. ²⁵ Looking ahead, the school expects to have about 920 students enrolled in grades ranging up to the third year of high school.

④All classes are taught in English and the school employs a cross-subject curriculum that leverages digital technology. ³⁰ Annual fees are about ¥8.5 million to ¥9.3 million, including dormitory fees.

⑤The headmaster said the school is based on the British

burgeoning 急に発展する
full-fledged 本格的な

proactive 先を見越して行動する

cross-subject curriculum 教科横断カリキュラム
leverage ～ ～を（巧みに）活用する

50

public school system, which sets it apart from Japan's other international schools.

35 ⑥More and more prestigious British schools are making inroads into Japan: Rugby School, which is known as the birthplace of rugby, is scheduled to establish a school in Kashiwa, Chiba Prefecture, in August, while Malvern College, which boasts more than 150 years of history, plans

40 to open an affiliated school in Kodaira, Tokyo, in September. ⑦"Britain has made the exporting of education a national strategy," said Manabu Murata, an international education commentator. "It's a strategy that has met the needs of Japanese parents, especially those with high incomes, who want

45 their children to receive a high-level education in English." ⑧The Education, Culture, Sports, Science and Technology Ministry does not keep track of the number of international schools in Japan, but Murata said there are at least 80 such institutions. (From The Japan News)

Rugby School ラグビー校

Kashiwa 柏市
Malvern College マルバーン・カレッジ

Kodaira 小平市

Manabu Murata 村田学氏

The Education, Culture, Sports, Science and Technology Ministry 文部科学省

 **While reading 1** 次に関して、記事を読んで分かったことをメモしましょう。

日本で近年開校されたインターナショナルスクール

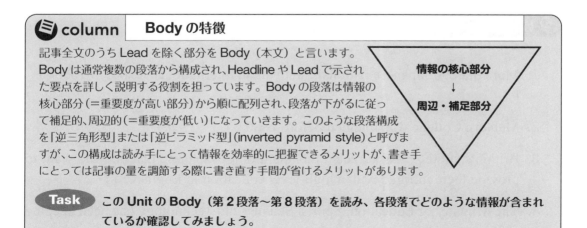

≡ column | **Body の特徴**

記事全文のうち Lead を除く部分を Body（本文）と言います。Body は通常複数の段落から構成され、Headline や Lead で示された要点を詳しく説明する役割を担っています。Body の段落は情報の核心部分（＝重要度が高い部分）から順に配列され、段落が下がるに従って補足的、周辺的（＝重要度が低い）になっていきます。このような段落構成を「逆三角形型」または「逆ピラミッド型」（inverted pyramid style）と呼びますが、この構成は読み手にとって情報を効率的に把握できるメリットが、書き手にとっては記事の量を調節する際に書き直す手間が省けるメリットがあります。

情報の核心部分
↓
周辺・補足部分

Task この Unit の Body（第2段落〜第8段落）を読み、各段落でどのような情報が含まれているか確認してみましょう。

1. 東北にインターナショナルスクールが開校した時期：[　　　]

2. 同校の寮費を含む学費：[　　　]

3. ラグビー校が系列校を開校した場所：[　　　]

4. 日本に存在するインターナショナルスクールの数：[　　　]

While reading 3　空欄に適切な単語または数字を入れ、記事の要約を完成させましょう。答えが単語の場合、最初の文字がヒントとして示してあります。

While no official record exists, it is said that there are at least ¹⁾_____ international schools in Japan. These schools are a growing ²⁾p_____ in the country amid burgeoning demand from parents seeking a full-fledged English-language education for their children. However, many such ³⁾i_____ are not regarded as "schools" under Japanese law, so their students do not qualify for Japanese ⁴⁾e_____ or junior high school diplomas. In an effort to obtain diplomas for their children, some parents temporarily enroll their kids in Japanese ⁵⁾m_____ schools.

While reading 4　3で空欄に入れた単語または数字が正しいか、音声で確認しましょう。

🔊 1-47

While reading 5　記事が示唆する内容と合致すれば T、しなければ F を記入しましょう。

1. More than 90 Japanese nationals study at an international school in Tohoku. [　　　]

2. Malvern College was founded before 1880. [　　　]

3. Britain's strategy has attracted the attention of Japanese parents who want to provide their children with a high-level education in English. [　　　]

4. The Ministry of Education, Sports, Science and Technology has been keeping official records of international schools in Japan. [　　　]

1. 専門家たちは政府に対し、子どもたちがインターナショナルスクールで受けた教育を評価す
るシステムを開発するよう要求している。

Experts have (on / to / called / develop / a system / the government) to
evaluate the education at international schools.

予 想 : ....

解 答 : *Experts have*

to evaluate the education at international schools.

2. ラグビー校はラグビーの生誕地として知られている。

Rugby School (as / is / of / known / rugby / the birthplace).

予 想 : ....

解 答 : *Rugby School* .

3. マルバーン・カレッジは2023年9月に小平市に系列校を開校する予定である。

Malvern College (in / to / open / plans / Kodaira / an affiliated school) in
September, 2023.

予 想 : ....

解 答 : *Malvern College*

in September, 2023.

4. 両親は彼らが英語で高いレベルの教育を受けることを望んでいる。

Parents (in / to / them / want / receive / a high-level education) English.

予 想 : ....

解 答 : *Parents*

English.

 **After reading 2** 次の説明はどの語についてのものか、文中から抜き出して必要に応じ正しい形に直しましょう。最初の文字がヒントとして示してあります。

1. to officially arrange to join a school, university, or course, or to arrange for someone else to do this

2. controlling a situation by making things happen rather than waiting for things to happen and then reacting to them

3. to link a group, a company or an organization very closely with another, larger one

4. the former students of a school, college, or university

5. a room for several people to sleep in, especially in a school or other institution

6. respected and admired as very important or of very high quality

1. e _____	2. p _____	3. a _____
4. a _____	5. d _____	6. p _____

After reading 3 次の課題について、自分の考えを述べましょう。

もし将来子どもができたら、子どもをインターナショナルスクールに入れたいと思いますか。またそう思う／思わない理由は何ですか。あなたの考えを書いてみましょう。

日本語でのメモ

英語での作文

UNIT 10

2-way plan hatched years ago takes Kuriyama, Ohtani to new heights

何年も前から準備した二刀流計画、栗山監督と大谷選手を新たな高みへ

 2023 年の WBC で日本は 3 大会ぶり 3 度目の優勝を果します。この Unit では、1 次ラウンド中国戦から決勝の米国戦まで全 7 試合に出場し、二刀流でチームを優勝に導いた大谷翔平選手と、それを支えた栗山英樹監督の絆について取り上げた記事を紹介します。

Before reading 1
説明を読み、内容に関する理解を深めましょう。
また表からどんなことが言えるか考えましょう。

-WBC（World Baseball Classic）はこれまで 2006 年、2009 年、2013 年、2017 年、2023 年の 5 回開催されています。

- 大谷翔平選手は 2013 年に北海道日本ハムファイターズ（Hokkaido Nippon-Ham Fighters）に入団し、プロとしてのキャリア（professional career）をスタートさせました。当時の日本ハムの監督（manager）は栗山英樹氏でした。

- その後、2018 年に大リーグ・アメリカンリーグ（American League）のロサンゼルス・エンゼルス（Los Angeles Angels）に移籍しました。

WBC の各大会における日米戦成績

回	日付	開催場所	ステージ	結果
1	2003.3.12	米国 アナハイム	第 2 ラウンド	3-4
2	2009.3.22	米国 ロサンゼルス	準決勝	9-4
3	（2013）	（対戦なし）	（対戦なし）	
4	2017.3.21	米国 ロサンゼルス	準決勝	1-2
5	2023.3.21	米国 マイアミ	決勝	3-2

Before reading 2
日本語に対応する英語表現を選択肢から選び、○で囲みましょう。

1. 指名打者　　　　　　designed hitter　/　designated hitter

2. 二刀流の選手　　　　two-way player　/　double-way player

3. 批評家　　　　　　　critic　/　criticalist

4. 救援　　　　　　　　relief　/　relievist

5. 先発投手　　　　　　started pitcher　/　starting pitcher

55

2-way plan hatched years ago
takes Kuriyama, Ohtani to new heights

①MIAMI — Los Angeles Angels superstar Shohei Ohtani was the starting pitcher against China, Japan's first opponent in this year's World Baseball Classic. He was also the designated hitter, batting third in the lineup, during the game at Tokyo Dome on March 9.

②Japan won that game 8-1 with Ohtani getting the win. He pitched four innings, giving up one hit with five strikeouts, while going 2 for 4 at the plate with two walks, a double and two RBIs.

③From the dugout, manager Hideki Kuriyama watched the two-way player and reportedly murmured, "Looks like he's turned out fine."

④Kuriyama was the manager of the Hokkaido Nippon-Ham Fighters when Ohtani started his professional career there in 2013. Together, they approached the challenge of making Ohtani a two-way player, a rarity in professional baseball.

⑤At the time, some critics said they were making a mockery of the game.

⑥Kuriyama first used Ohtani mainly as a pitcher. His plan consisted of Ohtani not playing in the game after he had pitched and not pitching in the game after he had batted.

⑦In 2016, Kuriyama employed Ohtani as a true two-way player. While paying close attention to any injury risks, he had Ohtani pitch and bat as the designated hitter in the same game.

⑧Ohtani moved to the Angels in 2018 and sought to stay as a two-way player in the major leagues.

写真：野球 WBC 決勝・米国戦 優勝し胴上げされる栗山監督（米フロリダ州で）
写真提供：読売新聞社
Shohei Ohtani　大谷翔平選手

Tokyo Dome　東京ドーム

2 for 4　4 打数 2 安打
RBI　打点（RBI は run(s) batted in の略）

Hideki Kuriyama　栗山英樹氏

make a mockery of ～
～をばかにする

⑨"Many fans have been supporting me" to be a two-way player, Ohtani said. "It's not something that belongs only to me anymore."

⑩Since then, he has overcome surgeries to his right elbow and left knee to become the MVP of the American League in 2021 and this year's WBC.

⑪In the past six years, Kuriyama had of course seen video of Ohtani, but hadn't had the two-way superstar play for him. Finally, Kuriyama could see with his own eyes how Ohtani has grown into the role they had started planning a decade ago.

⑫In Tuesday night's final against the United States, Ohtani came on in relief to close out the game in the ninth inning. He preserved Japan's 3-2 victory by striking out Angels teammate Mike Trout, the U.S. captain.

⑬Ohtani, who had dreamed of playing in the major leagues, and his manager Kuriyama, who helped prepare him for MLB, have spun a second chapter in their story after six years apart, culminating in a deserved championship. (From The Japan News)

Mike Trout　マイク・トラウト選手

 **While reading 1**　次に関して、記事を読んで分かったことをメモしましょう。

大谷翔平選手の二刀流選手としての歩み

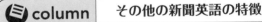

📋 column　｜ その他の新聞英語の特徴

新聞英語に見られるその他の特徴として、次の2つを挙げることができます。

① 発言者・報告者の名前は発言・報告内容の後に置かれることが多い。

例1：" ... ChatGPT ... had ... organization and composition," <u>the authors wrote.</u>

例2：" ... ChatGPT ... was somewhat repetitive," <u>Choi wrote.</u>

② 補足説明の挿入が多い。

例1：Jonathan Choi, <u>a professor at Minnesota University Law School,</u> gave ...

例2：" ... strategy," said Manabu Murata, <u>an international education commentator.</u>

これらの特徴は、限られたスペースの中で読み手が効率的に要点を把握できるよう配慮した結果生まれたと考えられます。

Task　Unit 2 の記事（Smiley, dimpled sphinx statue unearthed in Egypt）を読み、①の特徴が見られる部分に＿＿＿、②の特徴が見られる部分に ＿＿ を引きましょう。

⊗ While reading 2 記事の中で次の情報が述べられている段落の番号を書きましょう。

1. ワールド・ベースボール・クラシックでの日本の初戦の相手：[   ]

2. 大谷選手がプロ野球選手としてのキャリアをスタートさせた年：[   ]

3. 大谷選手がエンゼルスに移籍した年：[   ]

4. 決勝戦での米国代表の最後の打者：[   ]

⊗ While reading 3 空欄に適切な単語または数字を入れ、記事の要約を完成させましょう。答えが単語の場合、最初の文字がヒントとして示してあります。

When Ohtani started his professional career with the Hokkaido Nippon-Ham Fighters in ¹⁾_____, Kuriyama was the manager of the team. Together, they approached the ²⁾c_____ of making Ohtani a two-way player. In 2016, Kuriyama employed Ohtani as a true two-way player. He had Ohtani pitch and bat as the ³⁾d_____ hitter in the same game. In 2018, Ohtani moved to the Angels and sought to stay as a two-way player in the ⁴⁾m_____ leagues. At the WBC, Ohtani and his manager Kuriyama have spun a second chapter in their story after six years apart, culminating in a ⁵⁾d_____ championship.

⊗ While reading 4 3で空欄に入れた単語または数字が正しいか、音声で確認しましょう。

🔊 1-54

⊗ While reading 5 記事が示唆する内容と合致すれば T、しなければ F を記入しましょう。

1. Ohtani stood in the batter's box six times in the game against China.
[   ]

2. When Ohtani and his manager Kuriyama started their challenge, some commentators did not appreciate it. [   ]

3. In the 2013 season, Ohtani did not bat in the games when he was a pitcher.
[   ]

4. Ohtani played for the Hokkaido Nippon-Ham Fighters more than six years.
[   ]

1. 大谷選手はメジャーリーグで二刀流を貫こうとした。

Ohtani (as / in / to / stay / sought / a two-way player) the major leagues.

予想 ：

解答 ： *Ohtani*

                       the major leagues.

2. 過去 6 年、栗山氏は二刀流のスターには自身のためにプレーしてもらわなかった。

In the past six years, Kuriyama (for / had / him / play / hadn't / the two-way superstar).

予想 ：

解答 ： *In the past six years, Kuriyama*

                     .

3. 大谷選手は火曜日の米国との決勝戦でトラウト選手を三振させた。

Ohtani (in / out / Trout / struck / against / the final) the United States on Tuesday.

予想 ：

解答 ： *Ohtani*

                 the United States on Tuesday.

4. 大谷選手と栗山監督は 6 年ぶりに彼らの物語の第 2 章を紡いだ。

Ohtani and his manager Kuriyama (in / have / spun / after / their story / a second chapter) six years apart.

予想 ：

解答 ： *Ohtani and his manager Kuriyama*

                         six years apart.

After reading 2 次の説明はどの語についてのものか、文中から抜き出して必要に応じ正しい形に直しましょう。最初の文字がヒントとして示してあります。

1. a very famous performer, for example an actor, a singer or a sports player

2. someone who you try to defeat in a competition, game, fight, or argument

3. a situation in which the player who is supposed to be hitting the ball has to stop because he or she has tried to hit the ball three times and failed

4. someone whose job is to make judgments about the good and bad qualities of art, music, films, etc.

5. medical treatment of injuries or diseases that involves cutting open a person's body and often removing or replacing some parts

6. a person or group of people replacing others who have been on duty

1. s _____	2. o _____	3. s _____
4. c _____	5. s _____	6. r _____

After reading 3 次の課題について、自分の考えを述べましょう。

あなたが将来取り組んでみたいことは何ですか。またそれに取り組むために、どんな準備が必要だと思いますか。あなたの考えを書いてみましょう。

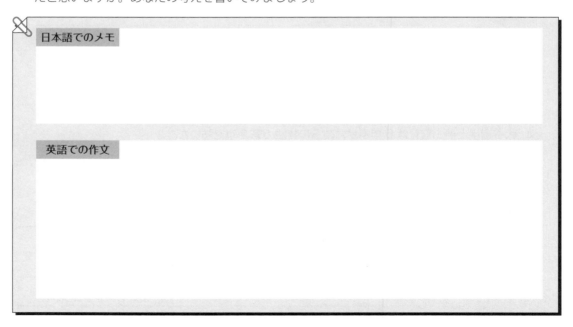

日本語でのメモ

英語での作文

Give and take: Clothing-swap services gain ground

ギブアンドテイクー服を交換するサービスが根づく

 みなさんは、必要な服と不要な服を交換できるサービスがあったら利用したいと思いますか。この Unit では、あるアパレルショップが服の廃棄を減らすために始めた服の物々交換サービスについて取り上げた記事を紹介します。

⊞ Before reading 1　説明を読み、内容に関する理解を深めましょう。
また図からどんなことが言えるか考えましょう。

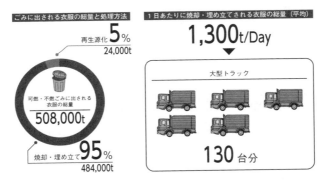

ごみに出される衣服の総量と処理方法
再生源化 **5**% 24,000t
可燃・不燃ごみに出される衣服の総量 **508,000t**
焼却・埋め立て **95**% 484,000t

1 日あたりに焼却・埋め立てされる衣服の総量（平均）
1,300t/Day
大型トラック
130 台分

出典：環境省ホームページ（https://www.env.go.jp/policy/sustainable_fashion/）

- 環境省（Environment Ministry）の推計（estimate）によれば、日本人が捨てる（throw away）衣服の量は一日平均で大型トラック 130 台分に上ります。衣類ごみ（clothing waste）の減少は国が対処する（address）べき喫緊の課題（urgent issue）の一つです。

⊞ Before reading 2　日本語に対応する英語表現を選択肢から選び、◯で囲みましょう。

1. 消費者　　　　　　　consumer / consignor

2. パーカー　　　　　　hoodia / hoodie

3. 大量廃棄　　　　　　mass disposal / mess disposal

4. 古着屋　　　　　　　firsthand store / secondhand store

5. 回収箱　　　　　　　collection box / correction box

Give and take: Clothing-swap services gain ground

①Stores and online platforms that facilitate clothing swaps are becoming increasingly popular. In recent years, consumers' behavior and mindsets have been changing, and more and more people are adopting eco-friendly lifestyles. Now, young people in particular appear to see clothes swapping as a convenient way to get their hands on desired items while recycling their unwanted apparel.

¥3,000 entrance fee

②One Sunday in early January, a pop-up clothing store, Closet to Closet, opened its doors in Shibuya Ward, Tokyo. Each "shopper" paid a ¥3,000 fee to enter the store, then placed three pieces of unwanted clothing into a collection box at the store entrance. They could then choose up to three "new" articles from among the more than 300 items on display, including coats and sweaters, but excluding underwear, shoes and children's clothing.

③The operator — Tokyo-based Energy Closet — describes itself as "an apparel brand that doesn't sell clothing."

④A woman in her 30s living in Tokyo took along items including a blouse and a knitted item and left with such pieces as a cardigan and a hoodie. "I wouldn't get much for my unwanted clothes if I took them to a secondhand store," she said. "Here, however, I can pick up various styles each time I come along and my unwanted clothes can prove useful to someone else."

⑤The store representative has been a fan of secondhand

写真：持ち寄った服と同じ数だけ交換できるコーナーがある店
写真提供：読売新聞社

pop-up　期間限定の

Closet to Closet　クローゼット・トゥ・クローゼット

Shibuya Ward　渋谷区

Energy Closet　エナジークローゼット

clothing since her student days and launched the business in 2019, after learning about the mass disposal of clothing. "I thought it would help reduce clothing waste if people could buy clothes while passing on their unwanted articles at the

35 same time," she explained.

⑥The representative has set up temporary Closet to Closet stores on more than 40 occasions nationwide, facilitating the swap of around 10,000 items of clothing.

40 **Reducing waste**

⑦A survey conducted last February by Geo Holdings Corp. — a Nagoya-based operator of secondhand stores — revealed that 81% of the about 1,600 respondents who had decluttered their homes said they had gotten rid of clothing.

45 Of them, 63% said they had sold their clothes at secondhand stores, the most popular means of clearing, followed by 60% of respondents who threw their items away.

⑧According to an Environment Ministry estimate, about 510,000 tons of the about 820,000 tons of clothes supplied

50 to Japanese consumers in 2020 will eventually be junked. Reducing clothing waste is thus an urgent issue for the nation to address. (From The Japan News)

Geo Holdings Corp.
ゲオホールディングス

⊗ **While reading 1**　次に関して、記事を読んで分かったことをメモしましょう。

1.　クローゼット・トゥ・クローゼットのシステム

....

2.　利用客の発言

....

3.　ゲオホールティングスの調査及びその結果

....

4.　衣服の廃棄に関する環境省の推定

....

記事の中で次の情報が述べられている段落の番号を書きましょう。

1. クローゼット・トゥ・クローゼットが期間限定で店舗を開設した場所：[   ]

2. 店舗の利用者のコメント：[   ]

3. 店の代表者が事業を始めた年：[   ]

4. 服の廃棄に関する環境省の推定：[   ]

空欄に適切な単語または数字を入れ、記事の要約を完成させましょう。答えが単語の場合、最初の文字がヒントとして示してあります。

According to an Environment Ministry estimate, about 510,000 tons of the about
1)_____ tons of clothes supplied to Japanese consumers in 2020 will eventually be junked. Reducing clothing 2)w_____ is thus an urgent issue for the nation to address. Under such circumstances, stores and 3)o_____ platforms that facilitate clothing swaps are becoming increasingly popular. Furthermore, in recent years, more and more people are adopting eco-friendly 4)l_____. Young people in particular appear to see clothes swapping as a convenient way to get their hands on desired items while recycling their 5)u_____ apparel.

3で空欄に入れた単語または数字が正しいか、音声で確認しましょう。

🔊 2-05

記事が示唆する内容と合致すればTを、しなければFを記入しましょう。

1. Young people are more likely to make use of clothes swapping. [   ]

2. A woman in her 30s living in Tokyo brought a cardigan and a hoodie to a Closet to Closet store. [   ]

3. The store representative has run the business for more than three years.
   [   ]

4. On average, one Closet to Closet store facilitates the swap of more than 300 items of clothing. [   ]

1. 女性はカーディガンやパーカーといった服を持って（店を）出た。

A woman (as / and / left / with / a cardigan / such pieces) a hoodie.

予 想 ：

解 答 ： *A woman*

a hoodie.

2. 経営者は約 10,000 点の衣類の交換を促進させてきた。

The operator has (of / of / clothing / facilitated / the swap / around 10,000 items).

予 想 ：

解 答 ： *The operator has*

3. 約 1,600 人の回答者の 5 分の 4 以上が服を処分したと述べた。

More than four fifths of the about 1,600 respondents (of / had / rid / said / they / gotten) clothing.

予 想 ：

解 答 ： *More than four fifths of the about 1,600 respondents*

clothing.

4. 若者は服の交換を、希望のアイテム入手のための便利な方法とみているようだ。

Young people (as / to / see / appear / clothes swapping / a convenient way) to get their hands on desired items.

予 想 ：

解 答 ： *Young people*

to get their hands on desired items.

65

 **After reading 2** 次の説明はどの語についてのものか、文中から抜き出して必要に応じ正しい形に直しましょう。最初の文字がヒントとして示してあります。

1. a situation in which you give something to someone and get another thing in return

2. someone's general attitude, and the way in which they think about things and make decisions

3. a piece of clothing with long sleeves that is worn over your clothes to protect them or to keep you warm

4. to remove things that you do not use so that you have more space and can easily find things when you need them

5. to get rid of something because it is no longer valuable or useful

6. to think about a problem or a situation and decide how you are going to deal with it

1. s＿＿＿＿＿	2. m＿＿＿＿＿	3. c＿＿＿＿＿
4. d＿＿＿＿＿	5. j＿＿＿＿＿	6. a＿＿＿＿＿

After reading 3 次の課題について、自分の考えを述べましょう。

もし近くに服の交換サービスを提供するお店があったとしたら、みなさんはお店を利用したいと思いますか。またそう思う／思わない理由は何ですか。あなたの考えを書いてみましょう。

日本語でのメモ

英語での作文

Company serves dried seaweed in the final frontier at JAXA's request

JAXA の要望に応え、企業が海苔を最後の開拓地へ提供

 みなさんはもし宇宙に行く機会ができたら、宇宙でどんなものを食べたいですか。この Unit では、江戸時代から続く老舗が JAXA の要望に応えるために宇宙で食べられる海苔を開発し、国際宇宙ステーションに届けられたことを報じた記事を紹介します。

Before reading 1

説明を読み、内容に関する理解を深めましょう。
また写真からどんなことが言えるか考えましょう。

- 宇宙食として認められるには、米航空宇宙局（National Aeronautics and Space Administration）が用いる HACCP [ハサップ] (Hazard Analysis Critical Control Points) という厳格な衛生管理システムの基準に従うことが求められます。

- 宇宙航空研究開発機構（Japan Aerospace Exploration Agency）は日本人宇宙飛行士 (Japanese astronauts) が宇宙空間で食べる「宇宙日本食（Japanese space foods）」を認証してきました。今回開発した海苔（nori seaweed）は国際宇宙ステーション (International Space Station) の外国人宇宙飛行士にも届けられました。

宇宙日本食の
スペースからあげくん

宇宙日本食の
森永ミルク生活

提供：JAXA   提供：JAXA

Before reading 2

日本語に対応する英語表現を選択肢から選び、〇で囲みましょう。

1. 完成、成就   culmination / cultivation

2. 食感   texture / textuary

3. 微生物   macroorganism / microorganism

4. 課長   section chief / subsection chief

5. 文書化   textation / documentation

Company serves dried seaweed in the final frontier at JAXA's request

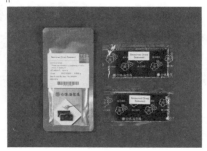

①Any company hopes its products are regarded as out of this world. For Yamamoto-Noriten Co., a Tokyo-based manufacturer of nori seaweed products that dates back to the Edo period, it's been there, done that.

②Seasoned nori dried seaweed that the company developed at the request of the Japan Aerospace Exploration Agency (JAXA) was delivered last year to a multinational crew of astronauts on the International Space Station (ISS).

③It marked the culmination of five years of research and development, and heralds what the company says is the start of an "era when astronauts from other countries eat traditional Japanese nori."

④JAXA has been carrying out a project to certify "Japanese space foods" for consumption by Japanese astronauts, with the aim of offering familiar tastes of home to help relieve stress in outer space.

⑤The products supplement the standard meals provided by the United States and other countries for astronauts aboard the ISS. In 2007, JAXA selected the first 29 of these "bonus meals" made by 12 food manufacturers.

⑥Currently, the selection includes 50 items from 28 sources*, ranging from yakisoba noodles to curry to yokan, a sweet red bean paste product.

⑦The space nori developed by Yamamoto-Noriten comes in a sealed package containing 10 sheets, and features the same refined flavor as the seasoned nori that the company produced for the first time in Japan in 1869.

写真：宇宙日本食の味付海苔
写真提供：JAXA

Yamamoto-Noriten Co. 山本海苔店

Edo period　江戸時代

bonus meals　ボーナス食

＊2023年1月時点。情報は随時更新され、2023年10月時点では31社/団体、52品目。
yakisoba noodles　焼きそば
yokan　羊羹

⑧Shinobu Soyano, 47, was in charge of development. In 2013, when he was a section chief in charge of sales and product development, Soyano was approached by JAXA, which said, "[Japanese] astronauts are telling us, 'We want

35 to eat mochi wrapped in nori in space.' Can you make it?"

⑨Soyano, who had never been involved with anything dealing with space, thought, "That would be great if they could eat it in space so far away." Readily accepting the challenge, he set out on development the following year.

40 ⑩The company manufactures its product under the standards used by the National Aeronautics and Space Administration (NASA), which are based on the stringent food safety system known as HACCP (Hazard Analysis Critical Control Points).

45 ⑪To be certified as a space food, it had to pass a battery of tests that, among other aspects, check for microorganisms or confirm the moisture content and texture after 18 months of storage. "The documentation was grueling, and I once had to write about 400 pages by myself," Soyano recalled

50 with a smile. (From The Japan News)

Shinobu Soyano 征矢野
忍さん

Hazard Analysis Critical
Control Points ハサップ
（総合衛生管理製造過程）

a battery of ～ 一連の～

grueling 厳しい

 While reading 1　次に関して、記事を読んで分かったことをメモしましょう。

1.　山本海苔店について

2.　「ボーナス食」に関する JAXA の取り組みについて

3.　宇宙で食べられる海苔の開発を担当した男性について

4.　HACCP 及びその試験に関して

While reading 2　記事の中で次の情報が述べられている段落の番号を書きましょう。

1. 山本海苔店の本社がある場所：[　　　]

2. 2007 年に JAXA が選んだ「ボーナス食」の品目の数：[　　　]

3. 山本海苔店が日本で初めて味付海苔を作った年：[　　　]

4. 開発を担当した男性が JAXA から依頼を受けた年：[　　　]

While reading 3　空欄に適切な単語または数字を入れ、記事の要約を完成させましょう。
答えが単語の場合、最初の文字がヒントとして示してあります。

JAXA has been carrying out a 1)p_____ to certify "Japanese space foods" for consumption by Japanese astronauts, with the aim of offering familiar tastes of home to help relieve 2)s_____ in outer space. The products supplement the standard meals provided by the United States and other countries for astronauts aboard the ISS. 3)S_____ nori dried seaweed that Yamamoto-Noriten Co. developed at the request of JAXA was delivered in 4)_____ to a multinational crew of astronauts on the International Space Station. It marked the culmination of five years of 5)r_____ and development.

While reading 4　3 で空欄に入れた単語または数字が正しいか、音声で確認しましょう。

🔊 2-12

While reading 5　記事が示唆する内容と合致すれば T を、しなければ F を記入しましょう。

1. The standard meals include Japanese space foods. [　　　]

2. Yamamoto-Noriten Co. has been producing the seasoned nori for more than 150 years. [　　　]

3. The man in charge of developing the space nori was in his late thirties when JAXA approached him. [　　　]

4. Shinobu Soyano started the development of the space nori in 2015.
[　　　]

語句を並べ替えて英文を完成させましょう。間違った場合、解答欄に正しい答えを書くこと。なお文頭に来る語句も小文字にしてあります。

1. 味付海苔は国際宇宙ステーションにいる海外の宇宙飛行士に届けられた。

Seasoned nori dried seaweed (of / to / was / delivered / astronauts / a multinational crew) on the ISS.

予 想 : ....

解 答 : *Seasoned nori dried seaweed*

.... *on the ISS.*

2. JAXA が選定したものは焼きそばから羊羹までに及ぶ。

(to / from / yokan / ranges / JAXA's selection / yakisoba noodles).

予 想 : ....

....

解 答 : ....

....

3. 宇宙海苔は 1869 年にその会社が作った味付海苔と同じ上品な風味が特徴だ。

The space nori (as / features / produced / the company / the seasoned nori / the same refined flavor) in 1869.

予 想 : ....

解 答 : *The space nori*

.... *in 1869.*

4. その基準は HACCP として知られる厳しい食品安全制度に基づいている。

The standards (as / on / are / based / known / the stringent food safety system) HACCP.

予 想 : ....

解 答 : *The standards*

.... *HACCP.*

1. the highest point or end of something, usually happening after a long time

2. to be a sign of something that is going to come or happen soon

3. to state that something is correct or true, especially after some kind of test

4. small amounts of water that are present in the air, in a substance, or on a surface

5. the way food or drink tastes or feels in your mouth, for example whether it is rough, smooth, light, heavy, etc.

6. the process of keeping or putting something in a special place while it is not being used

1. c _____	2. h _____	3. c _____
4. m _____	5. t _____	6. s _____

After reading 3 次の課題について、自分の考えを述べましょう。

あなたが「宇宙日本食」として海外の宇宙飛行士に食べてもらいたいものは何ですか。またその食べ物を選んだ理由は何ですか。あなたの考えを書いてみましょう。

日本語でのメモ

英語での作文

UNIT 13

Regulations may be eased on minpaku vacation rentals

民泊に関する規制を緩和へ

みなさんは民泊を利用したことがありますか。もしくは利用してみたいと思ったことはありますか。この **Unit** では、政府が民泊施設を運営する管理業者の用件を緩和する方針であることを報じた記事を紹介します。

🔲 **Before reading 1**
説明を読み、内容に関する理解を深めましょう。
また図からどんなことが言えるか考えましょう。

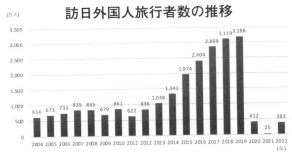

訪日外国人旅行者数の推移

出典：日本政府観光局（JNTO）

- 現行の規制（regulation）は住宅民泊事業法（Private Lodging Business Law）によって定められています。この法律は、民泊の管理会社（management company）に対し、不動産業への2年以上の実務経験や、宅地建物取引士（real estate transaction agent）などの資格（qualification）を求めています。

🔲 **Before reading 2**
日本語に対応する英語表現を選択肢から選び、○で囲みましょう。

1. 不動産　　　　　　　　real estate / joint estate

2. 省令　　　　　　　　　municipal ordinance / ministerial ordinance

3. 実務経験　　　　　　　moving experience / practical experience

4. 旅行代理店　　　　　　travel agency / travel insurance

5. チェックインの確認　　check-in confirmation / check-in confrontation

Regulations may be eased on minpaku vacation rentals

①The government will likely relax the requirements for management companies operating minpaku lodging businesses that rent condominiums or private homes to travelers, eliminating the requirement that their staff have practical experience or qualifications in the real estate business.

②The government's move is aimed at increasing the number of minpaku management companies and revitalizing the tourism industry in regional areas in anticipation of a recovery in the number of foreign tourists visiting Japan.

③The government will revise a Land, Infrastructure, Transport and Tourism Ministry ordinance as early as this summer.

④The Private Lodging Business Law requires that management companies be appointed to operate private accommodations that have more than five rooms and to be responsible for cleaning and check-in confirmations in the absence of the facility's owner.

⑤Under the current ministerial ordinance, the staff of management companies are required to have at least two years of work experience in the real estate business or a qualification such as being a certified real estate transaction agent. The revised ministerial ordinance will eliminate these requirements and instead require them to take a training program. The ministry will discuss the specific content of the training program based on the opinions of the Japan Association of Vacation Rental (JAVR) and will make it public as early as this fiscal year.

⑥Management companies for minpaku private

写真：コロナ規制緩和 宿泊客受け入れ再開に向け和室を清掃する
写真提供：読売新聞社

Land, Infrastructure, Transport and Tourism Ministry　国土交通省

Japan Association of Vacation Rental　住宅宿泊協会

accommodations are concentrated in urban areas. According to the JAVR, there were 2,993 such companies nationwide as of April 2022, with nearly 70% located in Tokyo, Osaka, Fukuoka and other major cities. While Tokyo has the
35 greatest number at 1,005, there are 13 prefectures that each have fewer than 10 management companies, including Aomori, Fukui and Kochi.

⑦The JAVR said that the existing strict requirements are a barrier to new entrants to the management industry. Currently,
40 minpaku management companies are mainly real estate companies. If the requirements are eased, it is expected that local hotels, inns and travel agencies will take on this role.

inn 旅館

⑧In rural areas, there are many old private homes and other facilities suitable for minpaku stays that are popular with
45 foreign tourists. However, when facility owners in rural areas try to outsource their facilities to management companies located in urban areas, they are often turned down or charged high fees because "routine cleaning is difficult." There have been many cases in which owners have given up on opening
50 minpaku accommodations because they could not find a management company. There have been increasing calls for the requirements to be eased. (From The Japan News)

⊗ While reading 1　次に関して、記事を読んで分かったことをメモしましょう。

1.　現行の住宅宿泊事業法の要件

....

2.　省令改正のねらい

....

3.　民泊施設の管理業者の分布状況

....

4.　住宅宿泊協会の指摘

....

記事の中で次の情報が述べられている段落の番号を書きましょう。

1. 省令の改正が予定される時期：[　　　　]

2. 国土交通省の省令の正式名称：[　　　　]

3. 現行の省令が要件として求めている実務経験の年数：[　　　　]

4. 民泊施設の管理会社に関する住宅宿泊協会のデータ：[　　　　]

While reading 3 空欄に適切な単語または数字を入れ、記事の要約を完成させましょう。答えが単語の場合、最初の文字がヒントとして示してあります。

In rural areas, there are many old ¹⁾p_____ homes and other facilities suitable for minpaku stays. However, many owners have given up on ²⁾o_____ minpaku accommodations because they could not find a management company there. Thus, the government will likely ³⁾r_____ the requirements for management companies operating minpaku lodging businesses as early as the summer of ⁴⁾_____. The government's move is aimed at increasing the number of minpaku management companies and revitalizing the tourism industry in regional areas in anticipation of a ⁵⁾r_____ in the number of foreign tourists visiting Japan.

While reading 4 3で空欄に入れた単語または数字が正しいか、音声で確認しましょう。

🔊 2-17

While reading 5 記事が示唆する内容と合致すればTを、しなければFを記入しましょう。

1. The government will revise the Private Lodging Business Law as early as the summer of 2023. [　　　]

2. The specific content of the training program will be announced in fiscal 2022 at the earliest. [　　　]

3. Less than 1,800 management companies for minpaku private accommodations were located in major cities in Japan as of April 2022. [　　　]

4. The revised ministerial ordinance will allow local hotels and inns to manage minpaku accommodations. [　　　]

語句を並べ替えて英文を完成させましょう。間違った場合、解答欄に
正しい答えを書くこと。

1. 政府は管理会社のスタッフに対する要件を撤廃するようだ。

   The government will likely (in / for / staff / eliminate / a requirement / the real estate business).

   予 想 ：

   解 答 ： *The government will likely*

                                                                      .

2. 政府の動きは、地方の観光業の活性化をねらいとしている。

   The government's move (at / in / is / aimed / revitalizing / the tourism industry) regional areas.

   予 想 ：

   解 答 ： *The government's move*

                              regional areas.

3. 改正した省令ではスタッフに講習の受講を要件とする見通しだ。

   The revised ministerial ordinance (to / take / will / require / the staff / a training program).

   予 想 ：

   解 答 ： *The revised ministerial ordinance*

                                                        .

4. 同省は早ければ年度内にも内容を公表する予定だ。

   The ministry (as / make / will / early / public / the content) as this fiscal year.

   予 想 ：

   解 答 ： *The ministry*

                  as this fiscal year.

1. a place in which someone lives or stays temporarily

2. the fact of seeing that something might happen in the future and perhaps doing something about it now

3. an order or rule made by a government or somebody in a position of authority

4. a piece of business that is done between people, especially an act of buying or selling

5. a rule, problem, etc., that prevents people from doing something, or limits what they can do

6. a small hotel or pub, especially an old one in the countryside

1. l _____	2. a _____	3. o _____
4. t _____	5. b _____	6. i _____

After reading 3　次の課題について、自分の考えを述べましょう。

あなたは民泊に関する規制が緩和されることに賛成ですか、反対ですか。また賛成／反対の理由は何ですか。あなたの考えを書いてみましょう。

日本語でのメモ

英語での作文

UNIT 14

Four-day working week 'more productive'—UK study

週4日労働、「生産性向上」―英実証実験

「1日8時間、週5日、週40時間」労働が「あたりまえ」の日本ですが、もし週4日労働になったらどうなるか、みなさんは考えたことがありますか？ この Unit では、週4日労働で生産性が向上したという英国での実証実験の結果を報じた記事を取り上げます。

 Before reading 1　説明を読み、内容に関する理解を深めましょう。
また図からどんなことが言えるか考えましょう。

- 週4日労働 (four-day working week) については、日本でもみずほフィナンシャルグループが 2020 年 12 月から「週休3～4日制」を導入しています。なお給与（salary）は勤務日数に応じて6～8割になります。
- 今回の研究では、労働時間の削減によって生産性 (productivity) が向上するだけでなく、疲労 (fatigue) の減少やスタッフの離職（staff leaving）の減少などの成果があったことが明らかになりました。

年間総実労働時間数（全国）

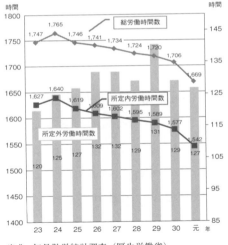

出典：毎月勤労統計調査（厚生労働省）

 Before reading 2　日本語に対応する英語表現を選択肢から選び、◯で囲みましょう。

1. 従業員　　　　　　　employee / employer

2. 燃え尽き症候群　　　burnup / burnout

3. 欠勤率　　　　　　　absenseeism / absenteeism

4. 歳入、収益　　　　　revenue / expenditure

5. 報酬　　　　　　　　reward / reword

79

Four-day working week 'more productive'—UK study

①A four-day working week is more productive for most staff and companies than the traditional five days, one of the biggest trials of its kind conducted in the UK reported on Tuesday.

②Over 60 firms in Britain took part in the six-month experiment allowing almost 3,000 employees to work one day less per week while retaining the same salary.

③Conducted between last June and December, it was organised by non-profit group 4 Day Week Global alongside the think tank Autonomy, the University of Cambridge and Boston College in the United States.

④It has been described as the world's biggest trial of a four-day working week.

⑤The study found more than nine out of ten firms will continue with the shortened working week or plan to do so, organisers said in a statement.

⑥Just four percent will not extend it.

⑦"Results are largely steady across workplaces of varying sizes, demonstrating this is an innovation which works for many types of organisations," said lead researcher and Boston College professor Juliet Schor.

⑧Productivity did not suffer from the lighter working weeks, with company revenue rising 1.4 percent on average over the trial.

⑨Revenue jumped 35 percent on average, when compared with similar periods from previous years.

⑩The study also found that hiring increased and absenteeism dropped — while the number of staff leaving fell sharply during the trial.

⑪In addition, researchers concluded that the overall health and well-being of employees had improved.

⑫Significant increases were observed in physical and mental

4 Day Week Global
4 デー・ウィーク・グローバル
think tank　シンクタンク
Autonomy　オートノミー

Juliet Schor　ジュリエット・ショアー氏

80

health, time spent exercising, and overall life and job satisfaction. ⑬Rates of stress, burnout and fatigue all fell, while problems with sleep declined, according to the statement.

35 — 'Really positive' —

⑭"In terms of employees, their mental health improved, they got better sleep, they got less burnt out," Cambridge University's Professor Brendan Burchell told AFP.

Brendan Burchell ブレンダン・バーチャル氏

⑮"But at the same time, the companies reported that if
40 there were changes in their profits or their performance, if anything they were more likely to go up rather than down."

⑯"And we got lots of very happy people — people really enjoyed it; they found it such a reward to have three-day weekends instead of two-day weekends."

45 ⑰UK environmental consultancy Tyler Grange was among 18 firms to adopt permanently the four-day week after taking part.

Tyler Grange タイラー・グレンジ

⑱"My experience has only been really, really positive — you can see it in people day-to-day at work, that they're more energized at work," Tyler Grange client director Nathan
50 Jenkinson told AFP.

Nathan Jenkinson ネイサン・ジェンキンソン氏

 **While reading 1** 次に関して、記事を読んで分かったことをメモしましょう。

1. 実証実験の概要

    ....

2. 従業員に起こった変化

    ....

3. Brendan Burchell 氏の発言

    ....

1. 実証実験に参加した企業の数：[　　　]

2. 実証実験参加後に週4日労働制を継続しないと回答した企業の割合：[　　　]

3. Juliet Schor 氏の発言：[　　　]

4. 実証実験参加後に週4日労働制の永続的な採用を行っている企業の数：[　　　]

While reading 3　空欄に適切な単語または数字を入れ、記事の要約を完成させましょう。答えが単語の場合、最初の文字がヒントとして示してあります。

According to a study conducted in the UK between June and December in 2022, a four-day working week is more $^{1)}$p_____ for most staff and companies than the traditional five days. Over 60 firms in Britain took part in the six-month experiment allowing almost $^{2)}$_____ employees to work one day less per week while retaining the same $^{3)}$s_____. The study found more than nine out of ten firms will continue with the shortened working week or $^{4)}$p_____ to do so. Productivity did not suffer from the lighter working weeks, with company revenue rising $^{5)}$_____ percent on average over the trial.

While reading 4　3 で空欄に入れた単語または数字が正しいか、音声で確認しましょう。

🔊 2-24

While reading 5　記事が示唆する内容と合致すれば T を、しなければ F を記入しましょう。

1. Many trials of a four-day working week in the UK involved more than 3,000 people.　[　　　]

2. A total of seven companies answered that they would stop a four-day working week.　[　　　]

3. Some small companies found a four-day working week as productive as the traditional five days.　[　　　]

4. More than 25 percent of the companies decided to adopt permanently the four-day working week after taking part in the experiment.　[　　　]

語句を並べ替えて英文を完成させましょう。間違った場合、解答欄に正しい答えを書くこと。なお文頭にくる語句も小文字にしてあります。

1. 週4日労働は伝統的な（週）5日（労働）よりもいくつかの会社にとってより生産性が高い。

(is / for / than / more productive / some companies / a four-day working week)
the traditional five days.

予 想：

解 答：

the traditional five days.

2. 6ヵ月間の実験によって、ほぼ3,000人の従業員が週1日少なく働くことができた。

The six-month experiment (to / less / work / allowed / one day / almost 3,000
employees) per week.

予 想：

解 答： *The six-month experiment*

per week.

3. 運動に使われる時間の顕著な増加が確認された。

Significant increases (in / time / were / spent / observed / exercising).

予 想：

解 答： *Significant increases*

.

4. 人々は週2日の代わりに週3日の週末を得られることがすてきな報酬であると気づいた。

People (it / to / have / found / three-day weekends / such a reward) instead of
two-day weekends.

予 想：

解 答： *People*

instead of two-day weekends.

After reading 2 次の説明はどの語についてのものか、文中から抜き出して必要に応じ正しい形に直しましょう。最初の文字がヒントとして示してあります。

1. a process of testing to find out whether something works effectively and is safe

2. money that you receive as payment from the organization you work for, usually paid to you every month

3. continuing or developing gradually or without stopping, and not likely to change

4. money that a business or organization receives over a period of time, especially from selling goods or services

5. relating to the health or state of someone's mind

6. the feeling of always being tired because you have been working too hard

1. t _____	2. s _____	3. s _____
4. r _____	5. m _____	6. b _____

After reading 3 次の課題について、自分の考えを述べましょう。

週4日制労働は日本でも機能すると思いますか。またそう思う／思わない理由は何ですか。あなたの考えを書いてみましょう。

日本語でのメモ

英語での作文

UNIT 15

Ukrainian officials visit Japan for landmine removal equipment demo

ウクライナ職員、地雷除去装置の視察で日本を訪問

 ロシアによるウクライナ侵攻が始まってから1年以上が経ちましたが、侵攻に伴い、多くの地雷が同国に埋設されました。このUnitでは、ウクライナ職員が地雷除去装置の視察のために日本を訪れたことを報じた記事を紹介します。

Before reading 1

説明を読み、内容に関する理解を深めましょう。
また表からどんなことが言えるか考えましょう。

JICAのウクライナ復旧・復興支援の重点4分野

今できる短期的な支援 ▶ ▶ ▶ ▶ ▶ 戦後を見据えた中長期的な支援

	分野	今できる短期的な支援	戦後を見据えた中長期的な支援
1	復旧に向けた基盤整備	地雷・不発弾対策、がれき処理 など	人材育成、復興開発計画
2	生活再建環境改善	電力などのインフラ復旧 など	インフラ再建
3	産業復興輸出促進	農業、起業家支援 など	経済・輸出の回復
4	民主主義ガバナンス強化	公共放送能力強化、金融改善 など	EU統合を見据えたガバナンス強化

出典：国際協力機構（JICA）

- ロシアの侵攻（Russian invasion）により、ウクライナ（Ukraine）の農地（farmland）等に無数の地雷（countless landmine）が埋設されました。同国の非常事態庁（emergency service）職員による地雷除去装置（demining equipment）の視察は、地雷除去作業（demining operation）による被害を減らすことを目的としています。

Before reading 2

日本語に対応する英語表現を選択肢から選び、○で囲みましょう。

1. 住宅地　　　　　　　　referential area ／ residential area

2. 悲劇　　　　　　　　　tragedy ／ tranquility

3. 不発弾　　　　　　　　unexploded bomb ／ disexploded bomb

4. 刺激、力　　　　　　　impetus ／ impediment

5. 環境整備、環境改善　　environmental redaction ／ environmental remediation

85

Ukrainian officials visit Japan for landmine removal equipment demo

①KOFU — Officials from the Ukrainian state emergency service visited Yamanashi Prefecture for a demonstration of equipment for clearing landmines manufactured by Nikken Corp.

②Countless landmines have been laid in Ukraine during the Russian invasion, even in farmland and residential areas, and deaths have occurred during demining operations.

③To prevent further tragedies, Ukrainians have high expectations for the technology developed by Nikken, a construction equipment manufacturer based in Minami-Alps, Yamanashi Prefecture.

④According to the Ukrainian agency, about 30% of the country, or 174,000 square kilometers, is likely to have been contaminated with landmines and unexploded bombs. However, the nation lacks enough mine removal equipment.

⑤At least 64 people have been injured and 13 killed during removals so far.

⑥"We're risking our lives to clear landmines," an official of the agency said.

⑦The company's demining equipment uses a roller-type cutter attached to the end of a heavy machinery arm that rotates at high speed to dig about 30 centimeters below the ground and detonate the mines.

⑧With the capability to demine 400 to 800 square meters per hour, the equipment allows mines to be cleared 20 to 100 times more efficiently than manually.

⑨Supported by the Japan International Cooperation Agency (JICA) and other organizations, nine Ukrainian officials learned about the demining equipment and operated it themselves at a Nikken facility in Hokuto, Yamanashi

写真：地雷除去の方法について説明を受けるウクライナ非常事態庁の職員ら
写真提供：読売新聞社
Ukrainian state emergency service　ウクライナ非常事態庁

Nikken Corp　株式会社日建

Minami-Alps　南アルプス市

detonate　爆発させる

Japan International Cooperation Agency　国際協力機構

Hokuto　北杜市

Prefecture, on Jan. 24.

⑩Ukraine's deputy director of explosive ordnance control said
35 that although training is necessary to operate the equipment,
it will be very useful and ensure the safety of personnel.

⑪A decision has been made to provide Ukraine with four of
the landmine detectors developed in Japan. However, the
provision of demining equipment has yet to be decided.

40 ⑫The Ukrainian government will consider requesting Japan's
assistance with the equipment based on the result of the officials'
trip.

138 units to 11 countries

45 ⑬The chair of the company saw people suffering as a result
of landmines when he visited Cambodia after the civil war,
and it was the impetus for him to start developing landmine
removal equipment.

⑭Since delivering the first unit to that country in 2000, the
50 company has exported a total of 138 units to 11 countries.

⑮The company is also focusing on environmental
remediation after mine clearance. In Cambodia, the
company cleared overgrown trees in tropical rainforest areas
and used heavy machinery to cultivate the soil and create
55 farmland. (From The Japan News)

deputy director of
explosive ordnance
control 爆発物対策副部
長

⊗ **While reading 1** 次に関して、記事を読んで分かったことをメモしましょう。

1. ウクライナにおける地雷の埋設状況

2. 日建が製造する地雷除去機の特徴

3. 日建が行っている地雷に関する取り組み

　記事の中で次の情報が述べられている段落の番号を書きましょう。

1. 日建の本社がある場所：[　　　　]

2. ウクライナにおいて地雷や不発弾処理の際に被害を受けた人の数：[　　　　]

3. 日建の地雷除去機が1時間で地雷を処理できる面積：[　　　　]

4. 日建がこれまでに輸出した地雷除去機の台数：[　　　　]

⊘ **While reading 3**　空欄に適切な単語または数字を入れ、記事の要約を完成させましょう。
答えが単語の場合、最初の文字がヒントとして示してあります。

According to the Ukrainian agency, about 30% of the country, or 174,000 square kilometers, is likely to have been contaminated with landmines and ¹⁾u_____ bombs and deaths have occurred during demining operations. To prevent further tragedies, ²⁾o_____ from the Ukrainian state emergency service visited Yamanashi Prefecture for a demonstration of equipment for ³⁾c_____ landmines manufactured by Nikken Corp. The company's demining equipment has the capability to ⁴⁾d_____ 400 to 800 square meters per hour, and allows mines to be cleared 20 to ⁵⁾_____ times more efficiently than manually.

⊘ **While reading 4**　3で空欄に入れた単語または数字が正しいか、音声で確認しましょう。

🔊 **2-31**

⊘ **While reading 5**　記事が示唆する内容と合致すれば T を、しなければ F を記入しましょう。

1. The area of Ukraine is larger than 800,000 square kilometers. [　　　　]

2. Nikken's demining equipment can remove explosive mines from more than 8,000 square meters per day. [　　　　]

3. The Ukrainian officials observed the use of the demining equipment when they visited a Nikken facility. [　　　　]

4. Nikken has been exporting landmine removal equipment for more than 20 years. [　　　　]

1. ウクライナの約30%（の国土）は地雷や不発弾に蝕まれている可能性がある。

   About 30% of Ukraine (is / to / been / have / likely / contaminated) with landmines and unexploded bombs.

   予 想 :

   解 答 : *About 30% of Ukraine*

   with landmines and unexploded bombs.

2. 日建が開発した地雷除去装置は職員の安全を確保するだろう。

   The demining equipment (by / will / ensure / Nikken / developed / the safety) of personnel.

   予 想 :

   解 答 : *The demining equipment*

   of personnel.

3. 日建の会長は地雷の結果人々が苦しんでいるのを目にした。

   The Nikken chair (as / of / saw / people / suffering / a result) landmines.

   予 想 :

   解 答 : *The Nikken chair*

   landmines.

4. カンボジアで、日建は土壌を耕して農地を作るために重機を活用した。

   In Cambodia, Nikken (to / and / used / cultivate / the soil / heavy machinery) create farmland.

   予 想 :

   解 答 : *In Cambodia, Nikken*

   create farmland.

 **After reading 2** 次の説明はどの語についてのものか、文中から抜き出して必要に応じ正しい形に直しましょう。最初の文字がヒントとして示してあります。

1. a bomb placed on or under the ground, which explodes when vehicles or people move over it

2. a very sad event or situation, especially one that involves death

3. to make a place or substance dirty or harmful by putting something such as chemicals or poison in it

4. to explode, or to make a bomb or other device explode

5. something that encourages a process or activity to develop more quickly

6. the process of improving something or correcting something that is wrong, especially changing or stopping damage to the environment

| 1. l _____ | 2. t _____ | 3. c _____ |
| 4. d _____ | 5. i _____ | 6. r _____ |

After reading 3 次の課題について、自分の考えを述べましょう。

ウクライナへの支援に関して、どんな取り組みが必要だと思いますか。またその取り組みが必要だと思う理由は何ですか。あなたの考えを書いてみましょう。

日本語でのメモ

英語での作文

90

UNIT 16

New research claims Leonardo da Vinci was son of a slave

新研究、レオナルド・ダ・ヴィンチは奴隷の息子と主張

「歴史上最も模写された作品」と言われる『最後の晩餐』や「世界で最も知られた美術作品」と言われる『モナ・リザ』を描いたことで有名なレオナルド・ダ・ヴィンチ。この Unit では、彼の母親は奴隷であったという新たな説を紹介した記事を取り上げます。

Before reading 1 説明を読み、内容に関する理解を深めましょう。
また年表からどんなことが言えるか考えましょう。

レオナルド・ダ・ヴィンチ略年譜

1452	イタリア・フィレンツェ郊外のヴィンチ村に生まれる
1466	「フィレンツェで最も優れた工房」と言われたヴェロッキオの工房に弟子入り
1472	「マスター（親方）」の資格を得て、父親のサポートで自分の工房をもつ
1482	イタリア・ミラノに移り、1494 年に「最後の晩餐」（1498 年完成）の制作を依頼するルドヴィコ・スフォルツァに仕える
1500	フィレンツェに戻り、1503 年から「モナ・リザ」の制作を始める
1508	ミラノに移り、解剖学の研究を始める
1513	イタリア・ローマに移り、「洗礼者ヨハネ」の制作を始める
1519	1516 年から滞在していたフランス・アンボワーズにおいて 67 歳で亡くなる

- レオナルド・ダ・ヴィンチ（Leonardo Da Vinci）の母親の奴隷（slave）説を主張（assertion）したのはナポリ（Naples）大学の Carlo Vecce 教授（professor）です。
- 従来、母親は小作農（peasant）のカテリナ・ディメオリッピと考えられていました。

Before reading 2 日本語に対応する英語表現を選択肢から選び、○で囲みましょう。

1. 公証人 　　　　　　　notary / notifier
2. 本部、本社 　　　　　branch / headquarters
3. 解放 　　　　　　　　emanation / emancipation
4. 博識家、大学者 　　　polyglot / polymath
5. 解剖学 　　　　　　　analogy / anatomy

New research claims Leonardo da Vinci was son of a slave

①Leonardo da Vinci, the painter of the Mona Lisa and a symbol of the Renaissance, was only half-Italian, his mother a slave from the Caucasus, new research revealed on Tuesday.

②Da Vinci's mother had long been thought a Tuscan peasant,
5　but University of Naples professor Carlo Vecce, a specialist in the Old Master, believes the truth is more complicated.

③"Leonardo's mother was a Circassian slave... taken from her home in the Caucasus Mountains, sold and resold several times in Constantinople, then Venice, before arriving in
10　Florence," he told AFP at the launch of a new book.

④"In the Italian city, she met a young notary, Piero (Peter) da Vinci, and their son was called Leonardo."

⑤The findings of Vecce, who has spent decades studying da Vinci and curating his works, are based on Florence city
15　archives.

⑥They have formed the basis of a new novel — The Smile of Caterina, the mother of Leonardo — while also shedding new light on the artist himself.

⑦Any new discovery about da Vinci is hotly contested by
20　the small world of experts who study him, but Vecce insists the evidence is there.

⑧Among the documents he found is one written by da Vinci's father himself, a legal document of emancipation for Caterina, to recover her freedom and recover her human
25　dignity.

— 'Spirit of freedom' —

⑨This document is dated 1452, and was presented Tuesday at a press conference at the headquarters of publishing house
30　Giunti in Florence.

Caucasus　カフカス

Tuscan　トスカーナ地方の

Carlo Vecce　カルロ・ベッチェ氏

Old Master　巨匠

Circassian　チェルケス人（白人で非インド・ヨーロッパ語族の種族）

Constantinople　コンスタンティノープル

Venice　ヴェニス，ヴェネツィア

Florence　フィレンツェ

Giunti　ジュント

⑩"It was written by the man who loved Caterina when she was still a slave, who gave her this child named Leonardo and (was) also the person who helped to free her," Vecce said.

⑪His assertion offers a radical change of perspective on da Vinci, who was believed to have been the product of an affair between Peter da Vinci and a different woman, young Tuscan peasant Caterina di Meo Lippi.

Caterina di Meo Lippi
カテリナ・ディメオリッピ

⑫Born in 1452 in the countryside outside Florence, da Vinci spent his life travelling around Italy before dying in Amboise, France in 1519, at the court of King Francis 1.

Amboise アンボワーズ
King Francis 1 国王フラ
ンソワ1世

⑬Vecce believes the difficult life of his migrant mother had an impact on the work of her brilliant son.

⑭"Caterina left Leonardo a great legacy, certainly, the spirit of freedom," he said, which inspires all of his intellectual scientific work.

⑮"Da Vinci was a polymath, an artist who mastered several disciplines including sculpture, drawing, music and painting, but also engineering, anatomy, botany and architecture."

⑯"He doesn't let anything stop him," Vecce said.

⊛ While reading 1 次に関して、記事を読んで分かったことをメモしましょう。

1. Leonardo da Vinci の父親について

....

2. Leonardo da Vinci について

....

3. Carlo Vecce 氏の発言

....

⊚ While reading 2 記事の中で次の情報が述べられている段落の番号を書きましょう。

1. Vecce 氏の所属：[   ]

2. Vecce 氏の記者会見が行われた場所：[   ]

3. トスカーナ地方の小作農 Caterina の名字：[   ]

4. Leonardo da Vinci が亡くなった年：[   ]

⊚ While reading 3 空欄に適切な単語または数字を入れ、記事の要約を完成させましょう。
答えが単語の場合、最初の文字がヒントとして示してあります。

Leonardo da Vinci is the painter of the Mona Lisa and a $^{1)}$s_____ of the Renaissance. Da Vinci's mother, Caterina, had long been thought a Tuscan $^{2)}$p_____, but according to the University of Naples professor Carlo Vecce, da Vinci was only half-Italian because she was a $^{3)}$s_____ from the Caucasus. The findings of Vecce are based on Florence city archives, which include a legal document of emancipation for Caterina. It was dated $^{4)}$_____ and written by Peter da Vinci, who was a young notary and helped to free her. Vecce's assertion offers a radical change of $^{5)}$p_____ on da Vinci.

⊚ While reading 4 3で空欄に入れた単語または数字が正しいか、音声で確認しましょう。

🔊 2-38

⊚ While reading 5 記事が示唆する内容と合致すれば T を、しなければ F を記入しましょう。

1. Leonardo da Vinci's father was Italian.   [   ]

2. Da Vinci's parents met in Constantinople.   [   ]

3. The legal document of emancipation for Caterina was written more than 500 years ago.   [   ]

4. Da Vinci lived over 70 years.   [   ]

語句を並べ替えて英文を完成させましょう。間違った場合、解答欄に正しい答えを書くこと。なお文頭に来る語句も小文字にしてあります。

1. ナポリ大学の教授は、真実がより複雑であると考えている。

(is / more / believes / complicated / the truth / the University of Naples professor).

予 想 : _____

_____

解 答 : _____

_____.

2. Vecce 氏の発見はフィレンツェ市公文書館の保管文書に基づいている。

The findings (of / on / are / based / Vecce / Florence city archives).

予 想 : _____

_____

解 答 : *The findings* _____

_____.

3. レオナルド・ダ・ヴィンチは Peter da Vinci とトスカーナの小作農の婚外子と考えられていた。

Leonardo da Vinci (to / was / been / have / believed / the product) of an affair between Peter da Vinci and a Tuscan peasant.

予 想 : _____

解 答 : *Leonardo da Vinci* _____

of an affair between Peter da Vinci and a Tuscan peasant.

4. 文書の中には Caterina の自由回復のために Peter da Vinci が書いたものもあった。

Among the documents (by / is / to / one / written / Peter da Vinci) recover Caterina's freedom.

予 想 : _____

_____

解 答 : *Among the documents* _____

recover Caterina's freedom.

1. someone who is owned by another person and works for them for no money

2. a poor farmer who owns or rents a small amount of land, either in past times or in poor countries

3. someone, especially a lawyer, who has the legal power to make a signed statement or document official

4. a place where a large number of historical records are stored, or the records that are stored

5. someone who goes to live in another area or country, especially in order to find work

6. someone who has a lot of knowledge about many diffirent subjects

1. s _____	2. p _____	3. n _____
4. a _____	5. m _____	6. p _____

After reading 3 次の課題について、自分の考えを述べましょう。

歴史上の出来事で知りたいと思うことは何ですか。またそのことについて知りたいと思う理由は何ですか。あなたの考えを書いてみましょう。

日本語でのメモ

英語での作文

Women still barred as Afghan universities reopen for men

アフガンで男性対象に大学が始業、一方で女性は依然禁止

みなさんは性別を理由に大学で学ぶことを禁止されたらどのように感じるでしょうか。この Unit では、アフガニスタンで大学が新学期を迎えたこと、一方で女性は大学へ行けない状態が続いていることを報じた記事を取り上げます。

Before reading 1

説明を読み、内容に関する理解を深めましょう。
また年表からどんなことが言えるか考えましょう。

- イスラム主義勢力のタリバン（Taliban）は、2021年夏にアフガニスタン（Afghanistan）で権力を握りました。
- タリバン当局 (authorities) による高等教育 (higher education) での性差別 (gender discrimination) は、世界の怒り (global outrage) を引き起こし (spark) ています。

アフガニスタンのイスラム主義組織タリバンの復権と女性の権利を巡る主な動き

2021年 8月	タリバンが首都カブールを制圧し、ガニ政権が崩壊
9月	タリバン暫定政権が発足。女性問題省が廃止され、勧善懲悪省を設置
	高等教育省が女性の教育を受ける権利の保障を表明
11月	勧善懲悪省がテレビ番組や映画の放送に関する指針を出し、テレビで女優が出演するドラマ放送などを禁止
22年 1月	教育省が中等学校の女子生徒の通学を3月に再開するとし、予定日当日に延期を発表
12月 20日	女性の大学教育を停止すると発表

出典：毎日新聞ニュースサイト

Before reading 2

日本語に対応する英語表現を選択肢から選び、○で囲みましょう。

1. 規制　　　　restoration / restriction

2. 親族　　　　relative / rerative

3. 廊下　　　　collider / corridor

4. 監禁　　　　imprisonment / inprisonment

5. 召使い　　　serpent / servant

Women still barred as Afghan universities reopen for men

①Afghan universities reopened on Monday after a winter break, but only men returned to class with a heartbreaking ban by the Taliban authorities on women in higher education still in force.

heartbreaking 胸の張り裂けるような

⁵ ②The university ban is one of several restrictions imposed on women since the Taliban stormed back to power in August 2021 and has sparked global outrage — including across the Muslim world.

③"It's heartbreaking to see boys going to the university ¹⁰ while we have to stay at home," said Rahela, 22, from the central province of Ghor.

Rahela ラヘラさん

Ghor ゴール

④"This is gender discrimination against girls, because Islam allows us to pursue higher education. Nobody should stop us from learning."

¹⁵ ⑤The Taliban government imposed the ban after accusing women students of ignoring a strict dress code and a requirement to be accompanied by a male relative to and from campus.

⑥Most universities had already introduced gender-segregated entrances and classrooms, as well as allowing women to be ²⁰ taught only by female professors or elderly men.

gender-segregated 性別によって分けられた

⑦Ejatullah Nejati, an engineering student at Kabul University, Afghanistan's largest, said it was women's fundamental right to study.

Ejatullah Nejati エジャトゥラ・ネジャティさん

⑧"Even if they attend classes on separate days, it's not a ²⁵ problem. They have a right to education and that right should be given to them," he said as he entered the university campus.

— **Government fear** —

⑨Waheeda Durrani, a journalism student in Herat until she ³⁰ was barred from the university last year, said the Taliban government wanted women to remain uneducated.

Waheeda Durrani ワヒーダ・ドゥッラーニーさん

Herat ヘラート

⑩"If Afghan girls and women get educated, they will never

accept a government that exploits Islam and the Koran," she said.

⑪"They will stand for their rights. That's the fear the government has."

⑫At the capital's private Rana University, male students trickled back to classes on Monday.

⑬"My sister, unfortunately, cannot come to the university. She is trying to study at home," said Ebratullah Rahimi, another journalism student.

⑭Posters dating from before the ban showing how women needed to dress were still on display in the university corridors.

⑮"I feel like a lesser human being," said Negah Khan, a university student from eastern Afghanistan.

⑯"When you have dreams but are subjected to imprisonment within the four walls of your house and made to serve people like a servant, it is disappointing."

⑰In an open letter, a group of women students urged male students and professors to boycott classes, one of the writers, Zahra Mandagar, told AFP.

⑱The Taliban group has invited only you to come to the classrooms . . . this is against our common aspirations to build a progressive, self-sufficient, free and equal Afghanistan, the letter said.

Koran	コーラン（イスラム教の経典）
Rana University	ラナ大学
Ebratullah Rahimi	エブラトゥラ・ラヒミさん
Negah Khan	ニガー・カーンさん
open letter	公開状
Zahra Mandagar	ザアラ・マンダガーさん

⊗ **While reading 1**　次に関して、記事を読んで分かったことをメモしましょう。

1. タリバン政権が行った規制

2. 多くの大学の対応

3. ジャーナリズムを専攻する学生たちのコメント

While reading 2

記事の中で次の情報が述べられている段落の番号を書きましょう。

1. タリバンが政権を掌握した時期：[　　　]

2. Rahela さんの年齢：[　　　]

3. Ejatullah Nejati さんが通っている大学：[　　　]

4. Ebratullah Rahimi さんの専攻：[　　　]

While reading 3

空欄に適切な単語または数字を入れ、記事の要約を完成させましょう。答えが単語の場合、最初の文字がヒントとして示してあります。

In Afghanistan, the Taliban stormed back to power in August ¹⁾_____ and its government imposed several restrictions on women. The university ban is one of the restrictions. The Taliban government imposed the ban after accusing women students of ignoring a strict ²⁾d_____ code and a requirement to be accompanied by a ³⁾m_____ relative to and from campus. Most universities had already introduced gender-segregated ⁴⁾e_____ and classrooms, as well as allowing women to be taught only by female professors or elderly men. The ban has sparked global ⁵⁾o_____, including across the Muslim world.

While reading 4

3 で空欄に入れた単語または数字が正しいか、音声で確認しましょう。

🔊 2-45

While reading 5

記事が示唆する内容と合致すれば T を、しなければ F を記入しましょう。

1. The university ban on women has been in force for more than four years.
   [　　　]

2. Many people all over the world are angry and shocked at the university ban on women. [　　　]

3. According to Rahela, Islam bans women from university education.
   [　　　]

4. No other universities in Afghanistan are larger than Kabul University.
   [　　　]

語句を並べ替えて英文を完成させましょう。間違った場合、解答欄に正しい答えを書くこと。なお文頭に来る語句も小文字にしてあります。

1. タリバン政権は女子学生に対し、厳格な服装規定を無視していると非難した。

(of / accused / ignoring / women students / the Taliban government / a strict dress code).

予想 : ....

....

解答 : ....

....

2. ほとんどの大学は女子が女性の教授や年配の男性の指導を受けられるようにした。

Most universities (be / by / to / women / taught / allowed) female professors or elderly men.

予想 : ....

....

解答 : *Most universities* ....

.... *female professors or elderly men.*

3. あなたは召使いのように人々に奉仕することを強制されている。

You (to / are / like / made / serve / people) a servant.

予想 : ....

解答 : *You* .... *a servant.*

4. 公開状で女性グループは教授に対して授業をボイコットするよう促した。

In an open letter, a group (of / to / urged / women / boycott / professors) classes.

予想 : ....

....

解答 : *In an open letter, a group* ....

.... *classes.*

 **After reading 2** 次の説明はどの語についてのものか、文中から抜き出して必要に応じ正しい形に直しましょう。最初の文字がヒントとして示してあります。

1. to be the cause of something, especially trouble or violence

2. to say that you believe someone is guilty of a crime or of doing something bad

3. to deliberately pay no attention to something that you have been told or that you know about

4. the job or activity of writing news reports for newspapers, magazines, television, or radio

5. to treat a person or situation as an opportunity to gain an advantage for yourself

6. a long narrow passage in a building, with doors that open into rooms on either side

1. s_____	2. a_____	3. i_____
4. j_____	5. e_____	6. c_____

After reading 3 次の課題について、自分の考えを述べましょう。

女性が高等教育を受けられるようにするために、どのようなことが必要だと思いますか。またそれが必要だと思う理由は何ですか。あなたの考えを書いてみましょう。

日本語でのメモ

英語での作文

¥300 bil. fund to help universities set up science faculties

理工学部の新設支援に 3,000 億円の基金

みなさんの専攻分野は文系と理系のどちらに分類されるでしょうか。この Unit では、文部科学省が、理工農系の学部を新設・転換する大学を支援するために、3,000 億円の基金を活用することを報じた記事を紹介します。

⊞ **Before reading 1**　説明を読み、内容に関する理解を深めましょう。
また図からどんなことが言えるか考えましょう。

- 日本では理系学部(science-related faculties)で学ぶ人材（human resources）の育成が急務になっています。
- 経済産業省（Economy, Trade and Industry Ministry)は、2030年にIT人材(IT professionals)の不足（shortage）が 80 万人近くに達すると推計して（estimate）います。

大学学部の学位取得者に占める理系の割合

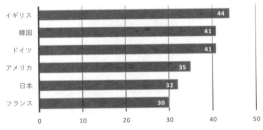

イギリス	44
韓国	41
ドイツ	41
アメリカ	35
日本	32
フランス	30

出典：文部科学省「諸外国の教育統計」令和 3（2021）年版に基づき作成

⊞ **Before reading 2**　日本語に対応する英語表現を選択肢から選び、○で囲みましょう。

1. 脱炭素　　　　　　　　dehydration / decarbonization

2. 停滞　　　　　　　　　stagnation / stagflation

3. 業績、実績　　　　　　true record / track record

4. 高等専門学校、高専　　college of technology / college of arts and sciences

5. 人件費　　　　　　　　personal expenses / personnel expenses

¥300 bil. fund to help universities set up science faculties

①A newly established subsidy program will be used to help universities establish about 250 science-related faculties to develop human resources in growth fields such as digital technology and decarbonization, according to sources.

5 ②A ¥300 billion fund created this fiscal year will be used to encourage private universities with many liberal arts departments to reorganize them to create science-related faculties over the next 10 years, the sources said. The Education, Culture, Sports, Science and Technology

10 Ministry intends to solicit applications for the subsidies from private and public universities.

③Payments would range from several hundred million yen to about ¥2 billion over a period of up to seven years, and subsidize such costs as launching new faculties or converting

15 existing ones.

④Applications are expected to be accepted for 10 years from March this year, and the ministry expects about 250 new and revamped faculties to be established through this initiative.

⑤If one new faculty was established at each of approximately

20 250 universities, that would mean one-third of the 721 private and public universities in Japan would receive the aid.

⑥National universities and colleges of technology will also be eligible for the subsidies, to foster work-ready highly specialized human resources in the information field,

25 according to the sources. The ministry envisages subsidizing about 60 such educational institutions with up to ¥1 billion for personnel expenses and facility maintenance, to increase the number of seats in faculties and graduate schools with a proven track record in fostering specialized personnel, the

30 sources said.

liberal arts department
文系学部

The Education, Culture, Sports, Science and Technology Ministry
文部科学省

work-ready　即戦力の

facility maintenance　施設整備

104

⑦The ministry currently provides private universities with subsidies every year, of which the total amount is equivalent to the new fund. It intends to change the current subsidy system to ensure stable university operations after science-related faculties are established.

⑧As an incentive for launching science-related faculties, the subsidies for private universities are set to be raised. Currently, the cost per faculty member and student in science-related faculties has been calculated the same way as for liberal arts faculties, but the amount will be set higher for science-related faculties. The ministry plans to implement these changes from fiscal 2023, the sources said.

⑨The ministry's move was spurred by the stagnation in Japan's development of human resources in science-related fields. University students majoring in science-related subjects account for only 17% of the total in Japan, lower than the average of 27% among members of the Organization for Economic Cooperation and Development.

⑩OECD countries have seen this number rise, but Japan's figure has barely changed.

⑪The Economy, Trade and Industry Ministry estimates that Japan will face a shortage of up to 790,000 IT professionals in 2030. (From The Japan News)

Organization for Economic Cooperation and Development 経済協力開発機構

⊗ While reading 1   次に関して、記事を読んで分かったことをメモしましょう。

1. 理系学部の新設・転換支援の対象となる大学等

....

2. 支援の内容及び期間

....

3. 文部科学省の動きの背景

....

1. 理系学部の新設・転換を促すために創設された基金の総額：[　　　　]

2. 理系学部の新設・転換を行う大学等への支援金額：[　　　　]

3. 日本国内にある私立・公立大学の数：[　　　　]

4. OECD 加盟国の大学で理系を専攻する学生の割合：[　　　　]

According to sources, a newly established ¹⁾s_____ program will be used to help universities establish about ²⁾_____ science-related faculties to develop human resources in growth fields such as ³⁾d_____ technology and decarbonization. Behind the move by the Education, Culture, Sports, Science and Technology Ministry was the ⁴⁾s_____ in Japan's development of human resources in science-related fields. For instance, university students majoring in science-related subjects account for only 17% of the total in Japan, and the ⁵⁾f_____ has barely changed.

🔊 2-51

1. According to the article, universities can make an application for the subsidies in 2030.　[　　　　]

2. The total amount of a new fund is almost the same as that of the annual subsidies provided to private universities.　[　　　　]

3. The average percentage of university students majoring in science-related fields in OECD countries is about 10% higher than the percentage of such students in Japan.　[　　　　]

4. The estimate by the Economy, Trade and Industry Ministry suggests that a lack of IT professionals will be a serious issue in Japan in several years.　[　　　　]

語句を並べ替えて英文を完成させましょう。間違った場合、解答欄に正しい答えを書くこと。なお文頭に来る語句も小文字にしてあります。

1. 3,000 億円の基金は私立大学が理系学部の創設促進に活用される予定だ。

A ¥300 billion fund will (be / to / to / used / encourage / private universities) create science-related faculties.

予想 : ....

解答 : *A ¥300 billion fund will*

create science-related faculties.

2. 国立大学はその補助金の資格対象になる見通しだ。

(be / for / will / eligible / the subsidies / national universities).

予想 : ....

解答 : ....

3. その数字は OECD 加盟国の平均である 27% よりも低い。

The figure (is / of / than / lower / 27% / the average) among the members of the OECD.

予想 : ....

解答 : *The figure*

among the members of the OECD.

4. 私立大学に対する毎年の補助金の総額は新基金に相当する。

The total amount of annual subsidies (is / to / for / equivalent / private universities / the new fund).

予想 : ....

解答 : *The total amount of annual subsidies*

....

 **After reading 2** 次の説明はどの語についてのものか、文中から抜き出して必要に応じ正しい形に直しましょう。最初の文字がヒントとして示してあります。

1. an amount of money that is collected and kept for a particular purpose

2. to ask somebody for something, such as support, money or information; to try to get something or persuade somebody to do something

3. to give money to somebody or an organization to help pay for something

4. to change something in order to improve it and make it seem more modern

5. the act of keeping something in good condition by checking or repairing it regularly

6. someone who works in a job that needs special education and training, such as a doctor, lawyer, or architect

1. f _____ 2. s _____ 3. s _____

4. r _____ 5. m _____ 6. p _____

After reading 3 次の課題について、自分の考えを述べましょう。

あなたは理系学部を増加させるという文部科学省の政策に賛成ですか、反対ですか。また賛成／反対する理由は何ですか。あなたの考えを書いてみましょう。

日本語でのメモ

英語での作文

Refugee from Taliban offers virtual tours of her homeland

タリバンからの（アフガン）難民、祖国のバーチャルツアーを開催

みなさんはアフガニスタンと聞いて何を連想しますか。多くが戦争やテロを連想すると思いますが、他方で、独自の文化や歴史、美しさも有しています。この Unit では、同国の魅力をバーチャルツアーで伝えようとする難民の取り組みを報じた記事を紹介します。

⊞ Before reading 1

説明を読み、内容に関する理解を深めましょう。
また図からどんなことが言えるか考えましょう。

- アフガニスタン（Afghanistan）から逃避する（flee）ことを余儀なくされた（forced）難民（refugee）の数は、2015 年段階で世界で 2 番目に多くなっていました。

- 上に加え、タリバン（Taliban）が 2021 年夏に政権を握った（took power）ことで、さらに多くの人々が国を離れました。国連人道問題調整事務所によれば、2023 年 1 月現在で、飢餓に直面している人々の数は 1,700 万人に上ります。

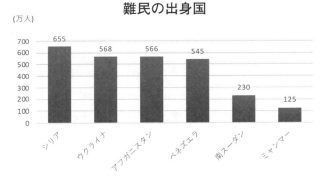

難民の出身国

（万人）

シリア	655
ウクライナ	568
アフガニスタン	566
ベネズエラ	545
南スーダン	230
ミャンマー	125

出典：UNHCR Global Trends 2022 を元に作成

⊞ Before reading 2

日本語に対応する英語表現を選択肢から選び、○で囲みましょう。

1. 売り上げ高、収益　　　　proceeds / proceedings

2. 要塞　　　　citadel / cityward

3. 侮辱　　　　insult / insultation

4. お見合い　　　　arranged marriage / communal marriage

5. 粘土　　　　clay / cray

Refugee from Taliban offers virtual tours of her homeland

①Forced to flee by the Taliban, Fatima Haidari now offers virtual tours of Afghanistan from her new home in Italy — with the proceeds funding secret English classes for women there.

②From her student flatshare in Milan, Haidari leads cyber-tourists around the western Afghan city of Herat, using Zoom to show them the grand mosque with its glazed tiles, the citadel and the bustling bazaar.

③The 24-year-old worked as a tour guide in Herat before fleeing when the Taliban took power in August 2021, and is now studying international politics at Milan's Bocconi university.

④But she remains passionate about showing outsiders the beauty of her country, even if few tourists currently dare visit.

⑤"When you hear about Afghanistan, you think of war, terror and bombs," Haidari told AFP in the little kitchen she shares with four other students.

⑥"I want to show the world the beauty of the country, its culture and its history."

⑦Organised through British tour operator Untamed Borders, the events draw people from Britain to Australia, Germany and India.

⑧A third of the money goes towards secret English classes for young women back in Afghanistan.

⑨The Taliban have imposed harsh restrictions on women since returning to power, including closing secondary schools and universities for girls and women.

⑩Haidari herself faced insults after becoming the first female tourist guide in Afghanistan.

⑪Local religious leaders accused her of doing the devil's work, particularly when accompanying men, while boys threw stones at her in the street.

Fatima Haidari　ファティマ・ハイダリさん

Herat　ヘラート

Bocconi university　ボッコーニ大学

tour operator　旅行業者
Untamed Borders　アンテイムド・ボーダーズ

— 'The power of our pens' —

⑫Haidari is passionate about education, after battling her whole life for access to books.

⑬Growing up in the mountains in the central region of Ghor, the youngest of seven children, her parents made her look after the sheep.

⑭"I would take the sheep out to graze by the river where the boys had school and secretly listen to their lessons," she recalled.

⑮"As I didn't have a pen, I would write in the sand or in clay."

⑯When she was 10, her impoverished family moved to Herat, where they could not afford to send her to school.

⑰For three years she worked at night on home-made items such as traditional clothes, to raise enough money to pay for classes and textbooks.

⑱She managed to persuade her parents to allow her to go to university in Herat, where she began studying journalism in 2019.

⑲"They wanted me to become a perfect housewife. But I didn't want to follow the same path as my two sisters and face an arranged marriage," Haidari said.

⑳In September last year, she joined around 20 refugee students welcomed by Bocconi University in Milan.

Ghor ゴール

impoverished 貧困に陥った

🕮 **While reading 1**　次に関して、記事を読んで分かったことをメモしましょう。

1.　Haidari さんが同国最初の女性ツアーガイドになるまで

....

2.　Haidari さんがアフガニスタンを脱出してから現在まで

....

3.　Haidari さんの発言

....

記事の中で次の情報が述べられている段落の番号を書きましょう。

1. Haidari さんの年齢：[   ]

2. 英国の旅行業者の名前：[   ]

3. Haidari さんの出身州：[   ]

4. Haidari さんが大学でジャーナリズムを学び始めた年：[   ]

While reading 3

空欄に適切な単語または数字を入れ、記事の要約を完成させましょう。
答えが単語の場合、最初の文字がヒントとして示してあります。

Fatima Haidari became the first female tourist guide in Afghanistan. In August
1)_____ the Taliban took power, and in September 2022, she joined around 20
2)r_____ students welcomed by Bocconi University in Milan and is studying
international politics there. But she remains passionate about showing outsiders
the 3)b_____ of her country. Organised through British tour operator Untamed
Borders, her 4)v_____ tours draw people from Britain to Australia, Germany
and India. A third of the money goes towards 5)s_____ English classes for
young women back in Afghanistan.

While reading 4

3 で空欄に入れた単語または数字が正しいか、音声で確認しましょう。

🔊 2-59

While reading 5

記事が示唆する内容と合致すれば T を、しなければ F を記入しましょう。

1. Sightseeing spots in Herat include the grand mosque and the citadel.
   [   ]

2. At present many people hesitate to travel to Afghanistan.   [   ]

3. Fatima Haidari has a total of six elder brothers and sisters.   [   ]

4. Haidari has spent more than one year in Italy.   [   ]

語句を並べ替えて英文を完成させましょう。間違った場合、解答欄に正しい答えを書くこと。

1. 貧困に陥っていた Haidari さんの家族は、彼女を学校へ送り出すための金銭的な余裕がなかった。

Haidari's impoverished family (to / her / not / send / could / afford) to school.

予 想 : ....

解 答 : *Haidari's impoverished family*

to school.

2. 彼女の両親は Haidari さんがヘラートにある大学に行くことを許可した。

Her parents (go / to / to / allowed / Haidari / university) in Herat.

予 想 : ....

解 答 : *Her parents*

in Herat.

3. Fatima Haidari さんは避難する前にヘラートでツアーガイドとして働いていた。

Fatima Haidari (as / in / Herat / before / worked / a tour guide) fleeing.

予 想 : ....

解 答 : *Fatima Haidari*

fleeing.

4. Haidari さんはヘラートにある要塞やにぎわうバザールをサイバー旅行者たちに見せるために Zoom を利用した。

Haidari (to / show / used / Zoom / cyber-tourists / the citadel) and the bustling bazaar in Herat.

予 想 : ....

解 答 : *Haidari*

and the bustling bazaar in Herat.

次の説明はどの語についてのものか、文中から抜き出して必要に応じ正しい形に直しましょう。最初の文字がヒントとして示してあります。

1. a flat square piece of baked clay or other material, used for covering walls, floors, etc.

2. a castle on high ground in or near a city where people could go when the city was being attacked

3. a market or area where there are a lot of small shops, especially in India or the Middle East

4. a weapon designed to explode at a particular time or when it is dropped or thrown

5. a remark or action that is offensive or deliberately rude

6. a type of heavy, sticky earth that can be used for making pots, bricks, etc.

| 1. t _____ | 2. c _____ | 3. b _____ |
| 4. b _____ | 5. i _____ | 6. c _____ |

次の課題について、自分の考えを述べましょう。

もしあなたのまわりに祖国から避難してきた人がいたら、その人にどんなサポートをしたいですか。またそのサポートをしたい理由はなんですか。あなたの考えを書いてみましょう。

日本語でのメモ

英語での作文

UNIT 20

Long lost Madagascar songbird seen again in wild

マダガスカルで「長きにわたり失われた」鳴鳥、野外で再び目撃

みなさんは鳥に興味がありますか？ 絶滅が危惧される鳥が世界に何種類いるか知っていますか？ この Unit では、長い間目撃情報がなく、絶滅が危惧された鳴鳥「ススケマダガスカルヒヨドリ」が数十年ぶりに目撃されたことを報じた記事を取り上げます。

Before reading 1 説明を読み、内容に関する理解を深めましょう。また図からどんなことが言えるか考えましょう。

- ススケマダガスカルヒヨドリ (dusky tetraka) は島国 (island nation) のマダガスカル原産 (native to Madagascar) で、1999 年の同国北東部の熱帯雨林 rainforest) での目撃が最後でした。
- この鳥は鳥 (類) 学者 (ornithologist) が絶滅 (extinction) を危惧していました。

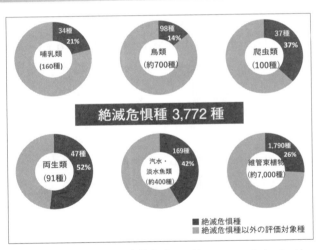

出典：環境省ホームページより作成（https://www.env.go.jp/content/900502268.pdf）

Before reading 2 日本語に対応する英語表現を選択肢から選び、○で囲みましょう。

1. （資源等の）保護論者 conservationist / conversationist
2. 探検 expedition / exploitation
3. 生物多様性 biaxiality / biodiversity
4. 熱帯林 tropical forest / evergreen forest
5. 外来種 invasive species / indegenerate species

115

Long lost Madagascar songbird seen again in wild

①Conservationists were celebrating Wednesday the first sightings in 24 years of the dusky tetraka, a yellow-throated songbird native to Madagascar for which ornithologists had feared the worst.

⑤②An expedition to remote regions of the island nation confirmed two recent sightings of the bird.

③Scientists also learned something about the petite bird's behaviour that could help explain how it escaped notice for so long, even if it remains extremely rare.

¹⁰④The last documented sighting of dusky tetraka, in 1999, was in the rainforests of northeastern Madagascar, one of the world's most diverse biodiversity hotspots with hundreds of unique vertebrate species.

⑤In December, an international team of researchers led by
¹⁵the US-based Peregrine Fund drove for 40 hours and hiked for half-a-day to the last spot the warbler-like bird had been seen.

⑥Much of the forest, they discovered, had been destroyed and converted to farms for vanilla production, even though
²⁰the area is officially protected.

⑦After eight days, team member John Mittermeier, director of the lost birds program at American Bird Conservancy, finally spotted one hopping through dense undergrowth on the ground near a rocky river and snapped a photo.

²⁵⑧"If dusky tetraka always prefer areas close to rivers, this might help to explain why the species has been overlooked for so long," he said.

— 'Data insufficient' —

³⁰⑨"Birding in tropical forests is all about listening for bird calls, and so you naturally tend to avoid spending time next to rushing rivers where you can't hear anything."

vertebrate 脊椎動物の

Peregrine Fund ハヤブサ基金
warbler 鳴鳥

John Mittermeier ジョン・ミッタマイヤー氏
American Bird Conservancy アメリカ鳥類保護協会

116

⑩Another dusky tetraka located by a second team also spent most of its time in dense vegetation close to a river, presumably looking for insects and other prey in the damp undergrowth.

⑪"Now that we've found the dusky tetraka and better understand the habitat it lives in, we can look for it in other parts of Madagascar," said Lily-Arison Rene de Roland, Madagascar Program director for The Peregrine Fund.

⑫The bird is on the Top Ten Most Wanted Lost Birds list, a collaboration between Re:wild, American Bird Conservancy and BirdLife International, all partners on the expedition.

⑬More than half of Madagascar's birds — some 115 species — are endemic, meaning they are found nowhere else.

⑭More than 40 of the island's bird species are classified as threatened with extinction on the Red List of the International Union for the Conservation of Nature (IUCN).

⑮The dusty tetraka — aka Crossleyia tenebrosa — is not classified for lack of data.

⑯The main drivers of biodiversity loss on Madagascar are forest destruction to make way for agriculture, habitat degradation, invasive species, climate change and hunting.

⑰About 40 percent of the island's original forest cover was lost between the 1950s and 2000, according to earlier research.

Lily-Arison Rene de Roland　リリー＝アリソン・レネイ・デ・ローランド氏

Madagascar Program director for The Peregrine Fund　ハヤブサ基金マダガスカルプログラムの責任者

Re:wild　自然保護に取り組む国際 NGO

BirdLife International　バードライフ・インターナショナル（鳥類の保護を目的とした国際環境 NGO）

International Union for the Conservation of Nature　国際自然保護連合

aka Crossleyia tenebrosa　ススケマダガスカルヒヨドリの学名

 **While reading 1**　次に関して、記事を読んで分かったことをメモしましょう。

1. dusky tetraka について

　　⋯⋯⋯⋯⋯⋯⋯⋯⋯⋯⋯⋯⋯⋯⋯⋯⋯⋯⋯⋯⋯⋯⋯⋯⋯⋯⋯⋯⋯⋯⋯⋯⋯⋯⋯⋯⋯⋯

2. 2 羽の dusky tetraka が発見された場所

　　⋯⋯⋯⋯⋯⋯⋯⋯⋯⋯⋯⋯⋯⋯⋯⋯⋯⋯⋯⋯⋯⋯⋯⋯⋯⋯⋯⋯⋯⋯⋯⋯⋯⋯⋯⋯⋯⋯

3. マダガスカルの生物多様性に関する状況

　　⋯⋯⋯⋯⋯⋯⋯⋯⋯⋯⋯⋯⋯⋯⋯⋯⋯⋯⋯⋯⋯⋯⋯⋯⋯⋯⋯⋯⋯⋯⋯⋯⋯⋯⋯⋯⋯⋯

While reading 2
記事の中で次の情報が述べられている段落の番号を書きましょう。

1. 最後に dusky tetraka が発見された年：[　　　]

2. John Mittermeier 氏の役職：[　　　]

3. マダガスカルに生息する鳥類の数：[　　　]

4. 1950 年代から 2000 年までの間にマダガスカルで失われた森林の割合：[　　　]

While reading 3
空欄に適切な単語または数字を入れ、記事の要約を完成させましょう。
答えが単語の場合、最初の文字がヒントとして示してあります。

The dusky tetraka is a yellow-throated songbird native to Madagascar. It was last documented in 1) _____ and was on the Top 10 Most Wanted Lost Birds list. In December 2022, an international team of researchers 2) d_____ for 40 hours and hiked for half-a-day to the last spot the warbler-like bird had been seen. After eight 3) d_____ of searching, a team member finally spotted one hopping through dense undergrowth on the ground near a 4) r_____ river. Then another dusky tetraka was found by a second team in dense vegetation close to a river. Through these findings, scientists have learned about where the 5) p_____ bird lives.

While reading 4
3 で空欄に入れた単語または数字が正しいか、音声で確認しましょう。

🔊 2-68

While reading 5
記事が示唆する内容と合致すれば T を、しなければ F を記入しましょう。

1. The dusky tetraka originally came from other African nations. [　　　]

2. Both of the warbler-like birds were found far from rivers. [　　　]

3. The Top Ten Most Wanted Lost Birds List was developed through a collaboration of three organizations. [　　　]

4. Madagascar's forested area less than halved in the latter half of the 20th century. [　　　]

 **After reading 1**　語句を並べ替えて英文を完成させましょう。間違った場合、解答欄に正しい答えを書くこと。

1. その鳥について学ぶことは、どうやってこれほどの長期間（鳥が）存在を気づかれなかったかの説明に役立つ可能性がある。

Learning about the bird (it / how / help / could / escaped / explain) notice for so long.

予想：

解答：　*Learning about the bird*

　　　　　　　　　　　notice for so long.

2. 研究者の国際チームはその鳥が最後に目撃された場所に半日かけて歩いた。

An international team of researchers (to / for / hiked / half-a-day / the bird / the last spot) had been seen.

予想：

解答：　*An international team of researchers*

　　　　　　　　　　　had been seen.

3. 森林の多くがバニラ生産用の農園に転用された。

Much of the forest (to / for / was / farms / converted / vanilla production).

予想：

解答：　*Much of the forest*

　　　　　　　　　　　.

4. もう一匹の鳥は川の近くの密生した茂みで時間を過ごした。

Another bird (in / to / time / close / spent / dense vegetation) a river.

予想：

解答：　*Another bird*

　　　　　　　　　　　a river.

 **After reading 2** 次の説明はどの語についてのものか、文中から抜き出して必要に応じ正しい形に直しましょう。最初の文字がヒントとして示してあります。

1. someone who works to protect animals, plants, etc., or to protect old buildings

2. a long and carefully organized journey, especially to a dangerous or unfamiliar place, or the people that make this journey

3. the variety of plants and animals in a particular place

4. a substance used to give a special taste to ice cream, cakes, etc., made from the beans of a tropical plant

5. an animal, bird, etc., that is hunted and eaten by another animal

6. a situation in which a plant, an animal, a way of life, etc., stops existing

1. c _____	2. e _____	3. b _____
4. v _____	5. p _____	6. e _____

After reading 3 次の課題について、自分の考えを述べましょう。

マダガスカルと同じ島国である日本にも多くの固有種が生息しています。固有種の絶滅を防ぐためにどんな取り組みが必要だと思いますか。またその取り組みが必要だと思う理由は何ですか。あなたの考えを書いてみましょう。

日本語でのメモ

英語での作文

英字新聞の見出しによく使われる単語

a	accord	名	協定、合意、一致 agreement, consent
	act	名	行為、動き activity, movement
	aid	名	援助 assistance
		動	援助する assist, help
	aim	名	目的、狙い purpose, object
		動	目的とする target
	air	動	発表する、表明する、意見を出す announce, voice
	assail	動	攻撃する、非難する attack, criticize
b	back	動	支援する support
	bag	動	捕らえる、手に入れる catch
	ban	名	禁止 prohibition
		動	禁じる forbid, prohibit
	bar	動	妨げる, 遮る refuse, shut out
	bid	名	企て、努力、提案 attempt, proposal
		動	要請する order
	blast	名	爆発、爆破 explosion
	blaze	名	火炎、火災 bright fire
	boost	動	(値段などを)押し上げる lift
	brief	動	要点を報告する sum up
c	charge	名	告訴 accusation
		動	とがめる、告訴する blame, accuse
	check	動	調査する examine
	cheer	動	声援する encourage
	cite	動	引用する quote
	claim	動	主張する demand
	clash	名	衝突 collision
	confab	名	会議 conference
	confer	動	会談する、協議する consult
	cop	名	警官 policeman
	crash	名	衝突、墜落 conflict, collision
	curb	名	制限、抑制 restraint
		動	拘束する、抑制する check
d	deal	名	取引、契約 arrangement, contract
	dip	動	(株価などが)少し下がる come down
	drive	名	運動 campaign
	due	名	予定 schedule

e	eye	動	目指す、もくろむ intend, hope
f	face	動	直面する confront
	fete	名	祝祭日 festival day
	fire	動	解雇する dismiss
	foil	動	挫折させる baffle
g	gain	名	利益、伸び、増進 increase, advance
		動	増加する increase
	grab	動	ひったくる、逮捕する clutch, arrest
	grill	動	厳しく尋問する question severely
h	hail	動	歓迎する、賞賛する acclaim, praise
	halt	名	停止 stoppage, suspension
		動	停止させる stop
	head	動	率いる、先頭に立つ、〜に向かう lead, precede
	hike	名	値上げ、上昇 increase, raise
		動	(価格を)上げる raise, lift
	hit	動	攻撃する、非難する attack, criticize
	hold	動	拘留する detain, take someone into custody
	hurt	動	傷つける injure, wound
i	ink	動	調印する sign a note, affix one's signature
	ire	名	怒り、憤怒 wrath, anger
	issue	名	論争 argument
l	lash	動	非難する attack, blame
	laud	動	称賛する praise
	launch	動	始める、着手する start, set about
	list	名	表 table
		動	名簿に記入する set forth
m	mar	動	損なう、傷つける damage
	mart	名	市場 market
	meet	名	会議、会合 assembly, meeting
		動	出会う encounter
	mishap	名	事故、災難 accident, disaster

	move	名	処置、行動、運動 movement
		動	動く turn
	mull	動	熟考する ponder
n	nab	動	ひったくる、逮捕する snatch, arrest
	name	動	指名する designate
	near	動	近付く approach
	net	動	捕える trap, snare
	nip	動	阻む、くじく block
	nix	動	否認する、不可とする disapprove
	note	名	公式文書 formal document
		動	気がつく、認める notice, perceive
	nuke	名	核兵器 nuclear arms
o	OK	動	承認する approve
	oust	動	追い出す expel
p	pact	名	条約、協定 treaty, agreement
	parley	名	協議、会談 discussion, conference
	peril	名	危険、危難 danger, hazard
		動	危険にさらす expose to danger
	pick	動	選ぶ choose
	plan	名	計画 project
	plea	名	嘆願 entreaty
	pledge	名	誓約 promise
		動	約束する、誓約する promise
	plot	名	陰謀 conspiracy
		動	陰謀を企てる conspire
	plunge	動	急落する drop (fall) suddenly
	poll	名	投票、世論調査 voting
	post	名	地位 position, station
	prexy	名	大学の学長 president
	probe	名	調査 investigation
		動	調査する investigate
	push	動	押し進める press, impel, drive
q	quake	名	地震 earthquake
	quell	動	鎮圧する suppress
	quit	動	辞める、去る give up, stop, leave
	quiz	名	質問 question
		動	質問する question, interrogate

r	rage	動	猛威を振るう be furious, be violent
	raid	名	侵略、急襲、手入れ attack
		動	襲撃する attack, assault
	rap	名	非難、叱責 censure, reproof
		動	非難する rebuke, blame, censure
	rift	名	割れ目、不和 discord, trouble
	rite	名	儀式 ceremony
	rock	動	激しく揺さぶる shake hard
	rout	動	大勝する win big, get an enemy on the run
	row	名	口論、不和、論争 quarrel
	rule	動	支配する govern, control
	rush	動	急ぐ speed, hasten, hurry up
s	score	動	扱き下ろす、非難する abuse (criticize) severely
	scrap	動	捨てる、廃棄する abandon, do away with, discard
	set	動	着手する、開始する set about, commence, decide
	slam	動	酷評する、非難する denounce
	slap	動	非難する reproach, rebuke
	slash	動	削除する eliminate, delete
	slate	動	予定する schedule
	slay	動	殺害する、惨殺する kill, slaughter
	snag	動	邪魔する、妨害する impede
	snub	動	無視する、はね付ける ignore, rebuff
	solon	名	米国の上院議員、下院議員 senator, representative or congressman
	split	名	分裂 division
		動	分裂する be disunited, be torn
	stab	動	刺す pierce, thrust
	stage	動	行う、計画する carry out
	stall	動	行き詰まる come to a standstill
	stem	動	食い止める、押える dam up, stop, check
	stir	動	動かす move, touch, inspire
	stress	動	強調する emphasize
	sue	動	訴える claim, tale to court
	suit	名	訴訟 lawsuit
	swap	名	交換 exchange
		動	交換する、交易する trade, exchange

t	**talks**	名	会談 negotiations
	test	名	検査、実験 experiment, trial
		動	実験する、試験する examine
	tie	名	関係 relation
	toll	名	代償、犠牲、死者数 fatalities, casualties
	tremor	名	地震 temblor, earthquake
	trim	動	削減する reduce, cut down
u	**up**	動	増大する、昇進させる increase, promote
	urge	動	要請する request, ask
v	**vex**	動	悩ます bother, worry, torment
	vie	動	競う、張り合う compete, contend
	vow	動	誓う swear
w	**wed**	動	結婚する marry, get married to
	win	名	勝利 victory
		動	打ち勝つ beat, defeat

新聞・雑誌によく出る略語

ADB	Asian Development Bank アジア開発銀行
AIDS	acquired immune deficiency syndrome 後天性免疫不全症候群、エイズ
ANA	All Nippon Airways 全日本空輸株式会社（全日空）
APEC	Asia-Pacific Economic Cooperation アジア太平洋経済協力
ASEAN	Association of Southeast Asian Nations 東南アジア諸国連合
BOJ	Bank of Japan 日本銀行
CEO	chief executive officer 最高経営責任者
CIA	Central Intelligence Agency 中央情報局（米国）
CO₂	carbon dioxide 二酸化炭素
DPRK	Democratic People's Republic of Korea 北朝鮮
EU	European Union 欧州連合
FAO	Food and Agriculture Organization 食糧農業機関（国連）
FBI	Federal Bureau of Investigation 連邦捜査局（米国）
FRB	Federal Reserve Bank 連邦準備銀行（米国）
GDP	gross domestic product 国内総生産
GMT	Greenwich Mean Time グリニッジ標準時
GOP	Grand Old Party 共和党（米国）（= Republican Party）
G8	Group of Eight (Major Industrial Countries) 先進8ヵ国
GWR	Guinness World Records ギネス世界記録
HIV	human immunodeficiency virus ヒト免疫不全ウイルス
IAEA	International Atomic Energy Agency 国際原子力機関（1957年発足）
IBRD	International Bank for Reconstruction and Development 国際復興開発銀行（通称World Bank [世界銀行]）
ID	identification 身分証明
IEA	International Energy Agency 国際エネルギー機関（OECDの下部組織、1974年設置）
ILO	International Labor Organization 国際労働機関（1919年設立）
IMF	International Monetary Fund 国際通貨基金（1945年発足）
IP	Internet Protocol インターネットプロトコル（コンピューターをインターネットに直接接続するためのプロトコル）
IQ	intelligence quotient 知能指数
IRA	Irish Republican Army アイルランド共和国軍（北アイルランドのカトリック系反英地下組織）
IWC	International Whaling Commission 国際捕鯨委員会
JAL	Japan Airlines Corporation 日本航空株式会社
JETRO	Japan External Trade Organization 日本貿易振興機構
JSDF	Japan Self-Defense Forces 自衛隊（日本）
JST	Japan Standard Time 日本標準時
LCC	Low Cost Carrier(s) 格安航空会社
LED	light-emitting diode 発光ダイオード
LSI	large-scale integration 大規模集積回路（コンピューター）
MRSA	methicilin-resistant staphylococcus aureus メチシリン耐性黄色ブドウ球菌
MVP	most valuable player 最優秀選手（野球）
NASA	National Aeronautics and Space Administration 航空宇宙局（米国）
NATO	North Atlantic Treaty Organization 北大西洋条約機構（1949年設立）
NG	no good 失敗
NGO	nongovernmental organization 非政府組織
NPO	nonprofit organization 民間非営利組織

ODA	Official Development Assistance 政府開発援助（日本）
OECD	Organization for Economic Cooperation and Development 経済協力開発機構
OHP	overhead projector オーバーヘッドプロジェクター
OPEC	Organization of the Petroleum Exporting Countries 石油輸出国機構
PLO	Palestine Liberation Organization パレスチナ解放機構（1974年から国連オブザーバー）
RBI	run(s) batted in 打点（野球）
ROK	Republic of Korea 大韓民国
RSPCA	Royal Society for the Prevention of Cruelty to Animals （英国）王立動物虐待防止協会（1824年設立）
SDI	Strategic Defense Initiative 戦略防衛構想（米国）
START	Strategic Arms Reduction Treaty 戦略兵器削減条約
TEPCO	Tokyo Electric Power Company 東京電力株式会社
TOEIC	Test of English for International Communication トーイック
TPP	Trans-Pacific Partnership 環太平洋連携協定
UN	United Nations 国連
UNCTAD	United Nations Conference on Trade and Development 国連貿易開発会議（1964年設立）
UNESCO	United Nations Educational, Scientific and Cultural Organization 国連教育科学文化機関、ユネスコ
UNHCR	United Nations High Commissioner for Refugees 国連難民高等弁務官事務所（1951年設立）
UNICEF	United Nations Children's Fund 国連児童基金（1946年設立）

UNIDO	United Nations Industrial Development Organization 国連工業開発機関
UNSC	United Nations Security Council 国連安全保障理事会
UNU	United Nations University 国連大学
VIP	very important person 重要人物
WHO	World Health Organization 世界保健機関（国連、1948年設立）
WTO	World Trade Organization 世界貿易機関（1995年発足）
WWF	World Wide Fund for Nature 世界自然保護基金（1961年 英国で発足）

日本の主要官庁名

内閣官房	Cabinet Secretariat
内閣府	Cabinet Office
防衛省	Ministry of Defense
総務省	Ministry of Internal Affairs and Communications
法務省	Ministry of Justice
外務省	Ministry of Foreign Affairs of Japan
財務省	Ministry of Finance Japan
文部科学省	Ministry of Education, Culture, Sports, Science and Technology
厚生労働省	Ministry of Health, Labour and Welfare
社会保険庁	Social Insurance Agency
農林水産省	Ministry of Agriculture, Forestry and Fisheries
経済産業省	Ministry of Economy, Trade and Industry
国土交通省	Ministry of Land, Infrastructure, Transport and Tourism
観光庁	Japan Tourism Agency
海上保安庁	Japan Coast Guard
環境省	Ministry of the Environment
警察庁	National Police Agency

TEXT PRODUCTION STAFF

| edited by | 編集 |
| Hiroko Nakazawa | 中澤 ひろ子 |

| English-language editing by | 英文校閲 |
| Bill Benfield | ビル・ベンフィールド |

| cover design by | 表紙デザイン |
| Nobuyoshi Fujino | 藤野 伸芳 |

| text design by | 本文デザイン |
| Ruben Frosali | ルーベン・フロサリ |

CD PRODUCTION STAFF

narrated by	吹き込み者
Howard Colefield (AmE)	ハワード・コルフィールド（アメリカ英語）
Carolyn Miller (AmE)	キャロリン・ミラー（アメリカ英語）

Meet the World 2024 English through Newspapers
メディアで学ぶ日本と世界2024

2024年1月20日　初版発行
2024年2月15日　第2刷発行

編著者　若有　保彦
発行者　佐野　英一郎
発行所　株式会社 成 美 堂
　　　　〒101-0052東京都千代田区神田小川町3-22
　　　　TEL 03-3291-2261　　FAX 03-3293-5490
　　　　http://www.seibido.co.jp

印刷・製本　(株)倉敷印刷

ISBN 978-4-7919-7289-0　　　　　　　　　　　Printed in Japan

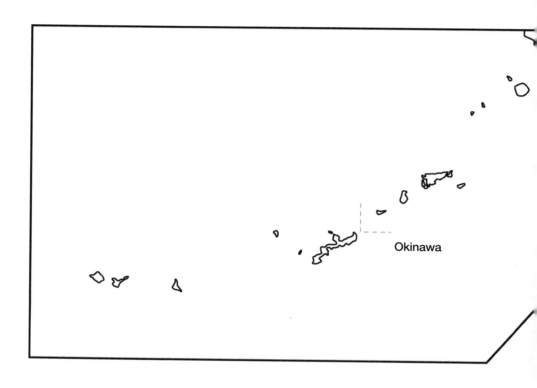

Okinawa

Ishikawa

Fukui

Toya

Tottori

Shiga

Shimane

Okayama

Hiroshima

Hyogo

Kyoto

Gifu

Saga

Fukuoka

Yamaguchi

Aichi

Nagasaki

Ehime

Kochi

Oita

Nara

Mie

Shizu

Kumamoto

Osaka

Miyazaki

Kagawa

Wakayama

Kagoshima

Tokushima